AMERICAN QUILT BLOCKS ★

★ 50 PATTERNS FOR 50 STATES ★

Beth Summers

American Quilter's Society

P. O. Box 3290 • Paducah, KY 42002-3290

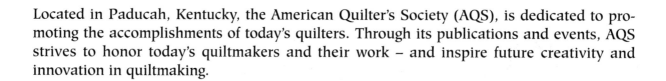

Located in Paducah, Kentucky, the American Quilter's Society (AQS), is dedicated to promoting the accomplishments of today's quilters. Through its publications and events, AQS strives to honor today's quiltmakers and their work – and inspire future creativity and innovation in quiltmaking.

Library of Congress Cataloging-in-Publication Data

Summers, Beth.
        American quilt blocks: 50 patterns for 50 states / Beth Summers.
            p. cm.
        ISBN 0-89145-861-1
            1. Quilting – Patterns.   2. Patchwork – Patterns.   3. United States –
Description and travel.
        I. Title.
        TT835.S824   1995   95-40904
        746.46–dc20   CIP

Additional copies of this book may be ordered from: American Quilter's Society,
P.O. Box 3290, Paducah, KY 42002-3290 @ $16.95. Add $2.00 for postage & handling.

Copyright: 1995, Beth Summers

Printed by IMAGE GRAPHICS, INC., Paducah, Kentucky

DEDICATION

This book is dedicated to my husband,
B.J. SUMMERS,
for his constant and unwavering love and support.

And to my mother,
SIGNE ANGELL GHOLSON,
for always encouraging me to develop and explore my talent.

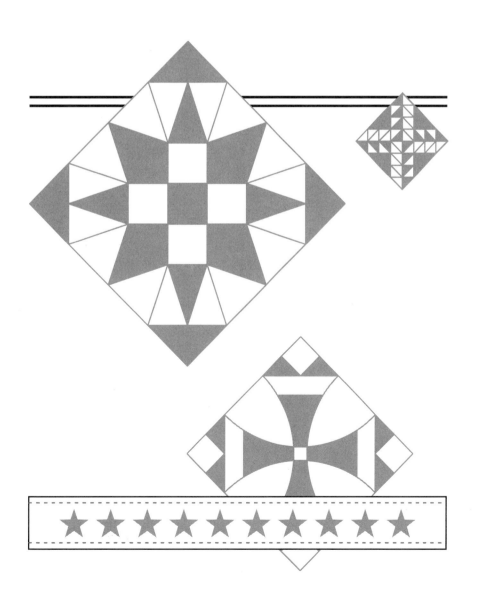

TABLE
of
CONTENTS

INTRODUCTION

I began working for the American Quilter's Society in the spring of 1988. Every year during the last week of April we all leave the offices at Schroeder Publishing to work a wild and hectic week at the AQS Quilt Show and Contest. Over the course of the past years I have had many jobs from stage building to selling merchandise at the AQS booth. But, for the past few years I have sold quilt books at the Museum of the American Quilter's Society to benefit the museum. While visiting, many quilters have shared ideas on what they would like to see in a book. The overwhelming theme seemed to be patterns, patterns, patterns! There were many requests for a pattern book that had a full-size design for each state in the United States. Because we didn't have one, I decided this was an opportunity worth exploring. The whole idea and purpose for the quilt show is to promote and inspire quilters, and yet, from what I hear, so many get intimidated by these gorgeous textile coverlets. But you don't have to be an expert to enjoy the hobby of quiltmaking! Women like my husband's grandmother had been designing and assembling quilts long before it was promoted to such a high-level art form. *Enjoy* this hobby, and if your points don't exactly meet or your quilting stitch isn't perfectly even, your project is still a very special artistic statement constructed by you! With each piece you complete, your skills will get better and better.

For each state in this book there is a full size 12" block pattern and an assembly diagram to aid in the piecing process. If there was a little extra room on the pattern page an outline of a state flower or tree leaf is included. These may be used for quilting patterns or embroidery as you see fit. There is also a quilt top example for each state. They are by no means the only way to handle each design, but are meant to give you an idea of how a quilt would look made with these blocks.

All 50 State Departments of Tourism were contacted as I began to gather information for this book. Most responded with a wonderful array of information and maps of their respective state. I would like to thank each for their time, effort, and materials.

Information was also gathered from: *World Book Encyclopedia*, past issues of *Fine Gardening* magazine, *Reader's Digest Encyclopedia of Garden Plants & Flowers*, *A Guide to the Most Familiar American Birds*, *The Bird Book – An Instant Guide to Birds, State Birds and Flowers, Identify Trees and Shrubs by Their Leaves – A Guide to Trees & Shrubs Native to the Northeast, A Guide to the Most Familiar American Trees, The Quilt ID Book*, and my own personal compilation of quilt block designs formed over the past thirty years.

Blocks were selected to give a good variety of patchwork designs. From star patterns and simple nine-patch styles, to curved designs, I wanted to provide a range of choices. I found that some states had a large list of blocks to choose from while others did not. So I used designs that were very easy to assemble and then hunted for just a few that would require more time and attention. I also took into account how these blocks would look when placed together to form a quilt top. Blocks that make a secondary design when assembled together seemed more interesting to me so these are the designs that were chosen. Hopefully, these will give a range of assembly challenges and be enjoyable as a finished project.

I hope you enjoy this pattern book and use it to expand your quilting hobby.

WE DARE
DEFEND
OUR RIGHTS

ALABAMA
The Heart
of Dixie

Alabama was the 22nd state admitted to the United States in 1819. This state has a profound historical reason for being known as the heart of Dixie. The Confederate Constitution was drawn up in Montgomery and that city became the first capital of the Confederate states. Traditionally this state had a "one crop" economy tied to cotton. But the area is also rich in minerals, and the state was quick to develop from agriculture to industry. The space center established in Huntsville boasts the world's largest collection of futuristic equipment, space exhibits, and missiles. The scenic Appalachian Mountains are found in the northeastern portion of this state, and a spectacular feature found here are the Cathedral Caverns. This cave system features the world's largest stalagmite and many unusual rock formations. The state's only seaport, Mobile Bay, is one of America's chief

ALABAMA

The name for this quilt pattern is simply "Alabama." It begins in the center with a simple Nine-Patch pattern and then radiates outward for three rows with squares the same width of the center blocks. The corners of these rows are the same pattern piece as the center blocks.

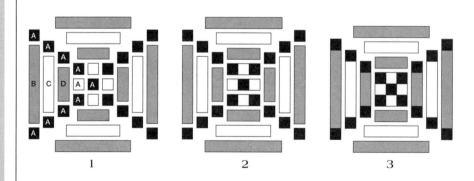

1   2   3

ASSEMBLY

Begin by laying out the pieces in this arrangement (1). Attach center squares A into strips (2). Then attach squares A to the ends of strips D, C, and B (3). Attach rectangle D to each side of the pieced center (4) then add the next sections DA (5). Attach rectangle C (6) and then add the next section CA (7). Then add rectangle B (8) and to finish the block add the last section AB (9).

QUILT TOP

Arrange the "Alabama" block with a light color 12" block between each and turn 45° on its tip to achieve this design. When you use this assembly the small darks squares within the block form a definite horizontal and vertical visual line.

harbors capable of handling over 30 ocean-going vessels at once. It is the state's second largest city and one of the nation's oldest. This city also celebrates Mardi Gras each spring along with New Orleans in Louisiana. The Azalea Trail, a famous 35-mile route, is also celebrated in the early spring. It passes by many beautiful homes and gardens and features azaleas and other colorful flowering shrubs native to this lush southern area. Bellingrath Gardens is a favorite tourist attraction just south of the city displaying flowers, shrubs, and trees in a distinctive setting.

■ The state flower is the hardy evergreen camellia. The glossy dark foliage is a verdant background for the pink, red, or white-bowl shaped blossom.

■ Southern pine is the state's tree, highly valued for paper pulp as well as lumber, resin, and turpentine.

■ This state's bird is the yellowhammer. Related to the woodpecker and sometimes called a golden-winged woodpecker, this bird grasps tree bark with feet adapted for the purpose and chisels out a niche for a nest.

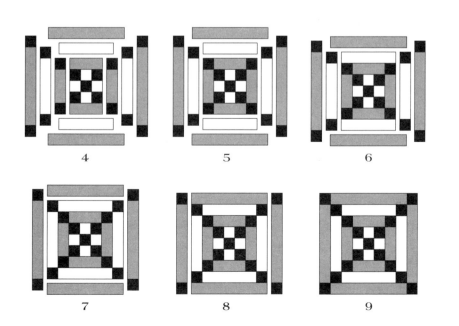

4 5 6

7 8 9

Alabama pattern – page 108

ALASKA
The Last Frontier

Alaska was the 49th state admitted to the United States in 1959. This is the largest state in the United States. It is more than twice the size of Texas, the second largest state in the nation, and yet it has the smallest population. Secretary of State William Seward led a movement to purchase this land from Russia in 1867 for about two cents an acre. He was heavily criticized and the area was nicknamed Seward's Folly. Then gold was discovered in Yukon Territory across the Alaskan border, and later in Nome and Fairbanks in the late 1800's. As a result, the state experienced a boom of prospectors and settlers to this beautiful but forbidding land. In 1968 huge oil and natural gas deposits were discovered in the Prudhoe Bay area, forever changing this state from Seward's Folly to a national treasure.

Sitka is the second oldest city in the state lying on the west coast of Baranof Island. It was the capital of the state from 1884 to 1900. The Sitka National Historical Park, famous for its 18 large totems, is a special tourist

ALASKA

This block is named "Alaska." It has a unique pieced Nine-Patch design in the center.

ASSEMBLY

Begin by laying out the pieces in this arrangement (1). Sew B and C pieces together and D and E pieces as shown (2). Attach A pieces to pieced sections BC and triangles F to pieced sections DE (3). Then sew these resulting pieced blocks together to make four pieced triangles (4). To complete this block sew these pieced triangles together (5).

QUILT TOP

Arrange the "Alaska" block side by side and top to bottom to achieve this design. When the sides of this block meet they form a new Four-Patch design that makes this a unique quilt top.

3

4

5

attraction here. Today's capital, Juneau, has a larger land area than any other city in the nation. Its location features steep mountains towering over a Pacific Ocean inlet. This picturesque area provides many tourist attractions. Eskimos along the Arctic coast follow old ways of life, hunting and fishing in kayaks, which reveals the lifestyle of a earlier culture. Ocean-going ferrys can navigate the state Marine Highway, a ferry system that makes accessible remote areas of the state. Alaska is famous for spectacular mountain scenery, and the highest peak in the U.S. is found here at Mount McKinley. The largest glacier in these northern mountains is the Malaspina Glacier on Yakutat Bay.

■ Forget-me-not, the state flower, grows wild all over the world. Species are found in damp meadows, beside brooks, and some make a blue carpet over mountain areas. They are an intense blue in color with a brilliant yellow eye in the center of five notched petals, and grow in clusters. This perennial is known as the symbol of friendship and true love.

■ The Sitka spruce takes its name from Sitka, Alaska, where it is a valuable lumbering tree.

■ Alaska's state bird is the willow ptarmigan, a member of the grouse group. This bird is famous for the ability to dramatically change its plumage from a varied chestnut brown in the summer to solid white in the winter. Its nest is a depression in the ground lined with bits of grass and leaves.

Alaska pattern – page 109

GOD
ENRICHES

ARIZONA
The Grand Canyon State

Arizona was the 48th state admitted to the United States in 1912. The Hopi Indians can be traced back to the 1100's in the settlement of Oraibi, and Geranimo led his warriors through this state until his surrender in 1886. Tombstone began as a famous silver mining town and was the site of the historic and infamous gunfight at the O.K. Corral. Here in the late 1800's Wyatt, Morgan, and Virgil Earp and Doc Holiday faced down Frank and Tom McLaury, and Billy and Ike Clanton. The pioneers who settled in south central Arizona realized that an ancient Indian civilization had once flourished at this site and named it Phoenix after the bird in Greek mythology of the same name that rises from its own ashes. Darrell Duppa, one of the settlers, predicted that a great city would one day rise on this site. Duppa was right, and today Phoenix is the state capital. It is filled with cultural facilities and historic residences. The Pueblo Grande Museum and Cultural

ARIZONA

This block is named "Arizona." While it has several pieces, it is simple to cut out and piece.

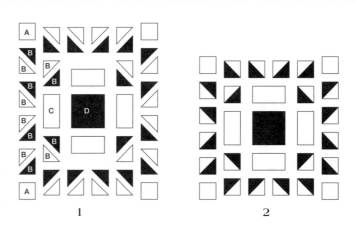

ASSEMBLY

Begin by laying out the pieces in this arrangement (1). Sew all B triangles together to make pieced squares (2). Attach these pieced blocks together as shown here (3). Then sew these pieced blocks together to make five strips (4). To complete this block sew these pieced strips together. (5)

QUILT TOP

Place the "Arizona" block on point at a 45° angle and insert a medium color 12" block in between each for this quilt top. Using popular southwestern colors in this quilt top will give you the southwestern ambiance of Arizona.

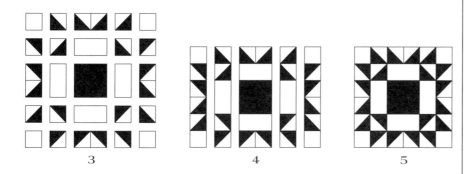

3   4   5

Park is a National Historic Landmark in the city and includes a Hohokam ruin and museum of this and other cultures of the southwest. Daily activities of Native American artists such as weaving, carving, sculpting and bead-working are demonstrated here. In the Painted Desert in northern Arizona the Petrified Forest National Park contains the most extensive and colorful concentration of petrified wood known in the world. The Grand Canyon National Park, one of the seven wonders of the world, runs along the edge of the Mohave Desert in the northwest corner of the state. The park consists of 250 miles of spectacular canyon formed by the Colorado river.

■ The blossom of the saguaro cactus is the state flower. It is the largest cactus growing in the United States. A height of 50 feet is not uncommon, and this desert plant lives up to 200 years in favorable conditions.

■ The paloverde is one of the most beautiful trees of the desert, blooming with small yellow flowers in April and May. It grows along the edges of desert canyons and its large seeds were once a food source for native Indians.

■ Arizona's state bird is the cactus wren, the largest member of the wren family. It has a distinctive white stripe over the eye and a white breast spotted with black. The prickly cholla cactus is their favorite place to build their nest, which is shaped like a flask lying on its side.

Arizona pattern – page 110

ARKANSAS

This block is named "Arkansas." The bordered edge surrounds a unique center block design.

ARKANSAS
Land of Opportunity

Arkansas was the 25th state admitted to the United States in 1836. The scenic Ozark and Ouachita Mountains cover the northwestern portion of this southern state. Its eastern border is the Mississippi River and the Arkansas River cuts through the heart of the state. Natural springs are plentiful, and the medicinal qualities believed to be in these waters have drawn people here since early times. Eureka Springs in the Ozarks has over 65 springs and is a Victorian settlement founded for the use of these waters. Mammoth Spring in Hot Springs has many natural mineral springs with the healing waters averaging a temperature of 145°. This city, founded on claims that bathing in these hot waters brings relief to physical ailments, is a health and pleasure resort in the Ouachita mountains. It is the only city in the nation with most of a national park within its city limits. Magnet Cove is an area in the foothills of the these mountains that has more than

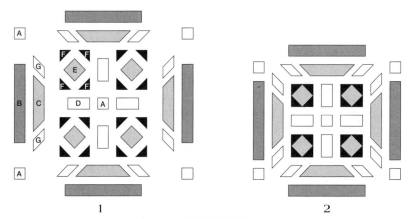

1   2

ASSEMBLY

Lay out the pieces as shown (1). Sew F triangles to E squares (2). Attach these to D rectangles and sew remaining D rectangles to center square A. Sew G pieces to C pieces and A squares to B rectangles (3). Attach the pieced GC sections together at the corners. Sew the three center pieced strips to make the center pieced square (4). Attach the pieced GC sections to the center block (5) then attach B rectangles to this center pieced square (6). To complete the block sew the AB strips to the sides (7).

QUILT TOP

Place the "Arkansas" block on point and insert a medium color 12" block in between each for this quilt top.

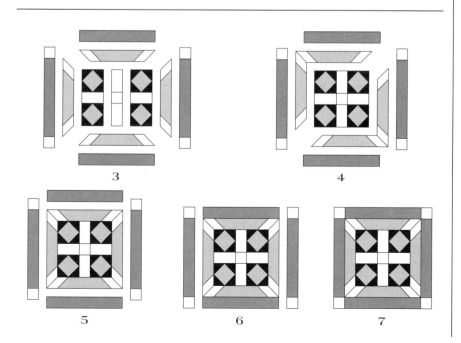

3

4

5

6

7

60 kinds of minerals. Crater of Diamonds, near Murfreesboro, is the only diamond field in the United States. The "Uncle Sam diamond" was unearthed here and has a value of $250,000. The Blanchard Springs Caverns draw many tourists to its unique and spectacular underground formations. The Ozark Folk Center close by features craft demonstrations and musical performances in a complex with an auditorium, shops, restaurant, lodge, and conference center. Some of the state's most famous and popular events are related to folk festivals and county fairs.

■ The apple blossom is the state flower.

■ The pine is the state tree for Arkansas. These trees are evergreen with needles that grow in groups of two to five. A woody cone is the fruit of this tree and it holds winged seeds within, releasing them as the cone matures and opens. These usually fast-growing trees are valued not only for their scenic beauty, but for their lumber and resins as well.

■ The mockingbird is the Arkansas state bird. It is clever at imitating other songbirds and can mimic a barking dog, insect noises, and some farm animals. These birds are plentiful in southern states and in the summer have been seen as far north as New York.

Arkansas pattern – page 111

CALIFORNIA

This block is named "California." It is a very bold and simple design that is fairly easy to assemble.

CALIFORNIA
The Golden State

California was the 31st state admitted to the United States in 1850. This state features several mountain ranges, level broad fertile valleys, vast severe deserts, and an ocean coastline that extends over 800 miles. Outdoor activities of all sorts are very popular because of the mild climate and spectacular landscape. The Tournament of Roses and the Rose Bowl Parade are held each year on New Year's Day in Pasadena, and the Disneyland amusement park is near Anaheim. San Francisco is built on steep hills facing water on three sides. To the west is the Pacific Ocean and to the east is San Francisco Bay, the largest natural harbor in the world. These two bodies of water are linked by the Golden Gate, a one mile channel. One of the world's largest suspension bridges, the Golden Gate Bridge, stretches across this

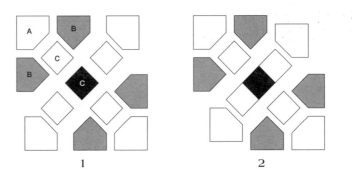

1   2

ASSEMBLY

Begin by laying out the pieces in this arrangement (1). Sew 3 C squares together as shown to make a strip (2). Then sew B pieces to the remaining C squares and A pieces to the ends of the center C strip (3). Attach the remaining A pieces to the BC sections (4). And finally sew these three sections together to complete this block.

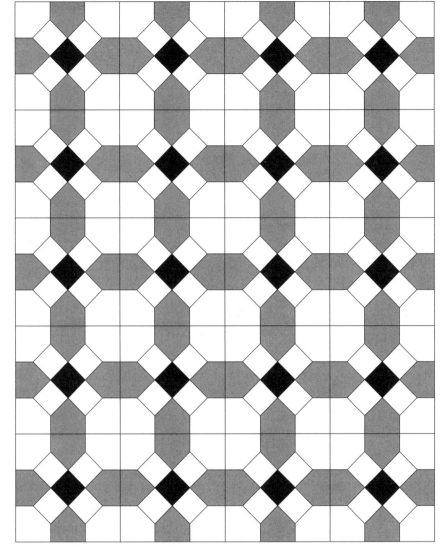

QUILT TOP

Place the "California" block side by side and top to bottom to achieve this quilt top design. The large pieces result in a very bold, striking arrangement.

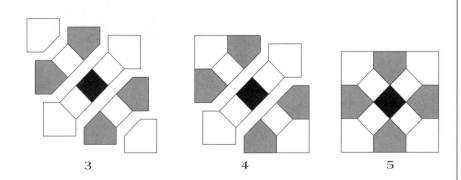

3   4   5

channel. Nob Hill, Chinatown, Russian Hill, and Fisherman's Wharf are a few of the colorful and cultural attractions of this city. San Diego is in the southwestern corner of the state near the Mexican border. Known as the "Cradle of Californian Civilization," it is now one of the nation's chief naval and aircraft centers. The San Diego Zoo has one of the largest collections of animals in the world. Los Angeles is the second largest city in the U. S. and is the chief business and trade center of the western part of the country. The mild climate and scenic beaches encourage an outdoor lifestyle here, and a natural extension of this is the Hollywood Bowl. It is an open-air theater famous for symphony programs and concerts. The movie industry got its start near Los Angeles in 1907 with the filming of *The Count of Monte Cristo*, and the motion picture capital of the world, Hollywood, is a district of this city.

■ The golden poppy is the state flower. It is brilliant yellow and two to three inches in diameter. The lengthy root system helps the plant to withstand long periods of dry weather.

■ The state tree is the California redwood. This magnificent forest tree is among the world's tallest living trees, growing from 200 to 275 feet in height.

■ The California valley quail is the state bird. Although it can fly, it seems to prefer walking. They build a grassy nest in a hollow in the ground next to a rock, stump, or similar shelter.

California pattern – page 112

COLORADO

This block is named "Colorado" and it is a very simple design that is easy to assemble.

COLORADO
The Centennial State

Colorado was the 38th state admitted to the United States in 1876. This Rocky Mountain state is absolutely filled to overflowing with varied and contrasting tourist attractions. Scenic mountain streams, rugged mountain peaks, ancient Indian ruins, and unique sandstone formations contribute to this state's unusual natural beauty. The Continental Divide runs through the Colorado Rockies and is a visual backdrop to the vast Great Plains region of eastern Colorado. Ancient cliff dwellings in Mesa Verde National Park are almost a thousand years old. Buffalo Bill's grave site atop Lookout Mountain is a reminder of Colorado's colorful western past. Gold was discovered in the Cherry Creek area in the 1850's and the resulting boom brought many prospectors and their families west. The community that developed as a supply point for prospector settlements came to be known as Denver. Another mining boom came to this city with the discovery of silver in the Rocky Mountains in the late 1800's.

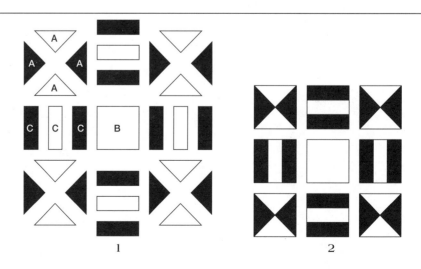

1

2

ASSEMBLY
Begin by laying out the pieces in this arrangement (1). Sew A triangles together as shown to make squares, then sew C rectangles to make squares (2). Sew these pieced squares together to form three strips (3), and then sew these strips together to finish the block (4).

QUILT TOP

Place a medium color 12" block in between each "Colorado" block and rotate all blocks 45° on point.

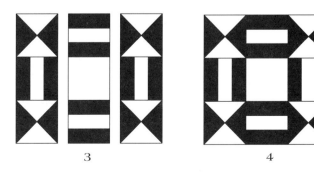

3

4

Aspen was once a prosperous silver mining town; it is today one of the most popular ski centers in the west featuring the world's longest chair lift. Although Colorado mines still produce gold and silver, oil has taken over as the state's most important mineral product. One of the most famous, though not the tallest, mountains in the Rocky Mountains is Pike's Peak. It is the center of one of the most popular mountain resort areas in America and maintains one of the highest meteorological stations in the world. The area of Garden of the Gods is at the eastern base of the Rocky Mountains near Colorado Springs. It is a collection of massive red and white sandstone rock formations and is the site of now famous sunrise services on Easter Sunday.

■ Rocky Mountain columbine, a large blue-and-white perennial with a blossom measuring two inches across is honored as the state flower. The leaf arrangement is reminiscent of a maidenhair fern.

■ The state tree is the blue spruce.

■ The lark bunting is the state bird. It is similar to the European skylark in that it will sing as it soars in the sky. These birds are seed-eaters and prefer to nest on the ground. They build their homes from an outer layer of grass and weed stems and then line it with down from plants.

Colorado pattern – page 113

HE WHO
TRANSPLANTED
STILL SUSTAINES

CONNECTICUT
The Constitution State

Connecticut became the 5th state admitted to the United States in 1788. This state has an Atlantic coastline with many fine harbors. Some ocean-going vessels can even sail up the Connecticut River as far north as Hartford. Long Island, part of New York, helps protect Connecticut's shoreline and salt marshes from ocean storms. The capital of Hartford is known as the Insurance City because so many insurance companies have their headquarters here. Yale University in New Haven is the third oldest U. S. university and the Yale University Art Gallery exhibits rare and exquisite artifacts. Eli Whitney's inventions in the city of Hamden directly contributed to the manufacturing might of this tiny state. Today it is a leader in the production of helicopter and jet engines, and submarines. The first atomic submarine, the *Nautilus*, was built at Groton and launched in 1954. Tobacco is this state's leading field crop and is unique because it is grown in the shade for use as outer wrappings for cigars.

CONNECTICUT

This block is named "Connecticut," and what a great pattern it is. With only one pattern piece, you can dig into your scrap pile and make a beautiful quilt.

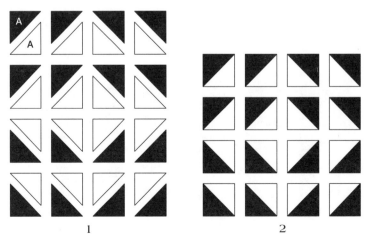

ASSEMBLY

Begin by laying out the pieces for this block in this arrangement (1). Sew A triangles together as shown to make squares (2). Then sew these pieced squares together to form 4 strips (3). To finish the block sew these 4 strips together (4).

QUILT TOP

Placing the blocks side by side and top to bottom will give you this design. There are many possibilities for this design by using different color triangles in each block.

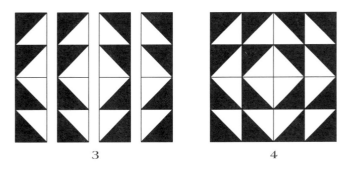

3   4

This makes it the most expensive tobacco in the nation. One of America's most beautiful forests, Cathedral Pines in Cornwall, is a white pine woodland. The trees grow so thickly here that it is said sunlight rarely reaches the forest floor in places. Historic buildings and early New England culture are a popular tourist draw to this small state. The Nathan Hale Homestead in South Coventry celebrates the life of this patriot. The American Shakespeare Festival lasts from August to October in Stratford and Connecticut's seafaring culture is well represented in Mystic Seaport, a renovated whaling village of the 1800's. The whaling ship *Charles W. Morgan*, and a square-rigged 1882 training ship the *Joseph Conrad,* are two vessels displayed in the harbor at this popular tourist attraction. Each year during the second week in August the Mystic Outdoor Art Festival provides an opportunity to view and purchase fine arts and crafts of the state.

■ Mountain laurel is the state flower. This beautiful, evergreen shrub may grow to fifteen feet or more in height, but will bloom when it is quite small.

■ The state tree is the White Oak.

■ Connecticut claims the robin as the state bird.

Connecticut pattern – page 114

DELAWARE
The First
State

Delaware was the 1st state. This state voted to unanimously ratify the United States Constitution on December 7, 1787, and was the first state to do so. A Swedish expedition was the first permanent colony and built the first log cabins in America. Because it is easier and less expensive for companies to incorporate in this state, several of the nation's largest corporations have their headquarters here. The only smaller state in the union is Rhode Island, and yet Delaware ranks as one of the leading broiler chicken-raising states. Sussex County in southern Delaware is one of the richest farm regions in the nation because of the chickens raised here. The New Castle Historical Society exhibits arts, crafts, and furnishings from the early 1700's in Amstel House. Covering 185 acres, the Hagley Museum Historic Site and Museum

DELAWARE

This block is named "Delaware." It is a little involved to assemble, but the curved pieces make it unusual.

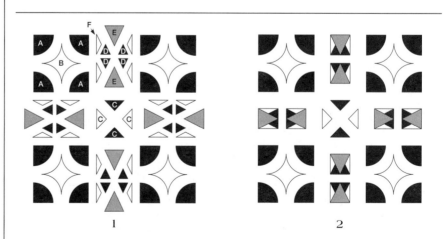

1   2

ASSEMBLY

Begin by laying out the pieces for each quarter of this block in this arrangement (1). Sew E, F, and D pieces together as shown (2). Then sew these segments together. Join center triangles C together to form the center square (3). Sew A pieces to B pieces to form 4 squares (4) and then sew these pieced segments into three strips (5). Join these three strips together to finish the block (6).

QUILT TOP

Placing the "Delaware" blocks side by side and top to bottom will give you this quilt top arrangement. When joined in this manner a design develops that looks like a pieced sashing across the quilt top.

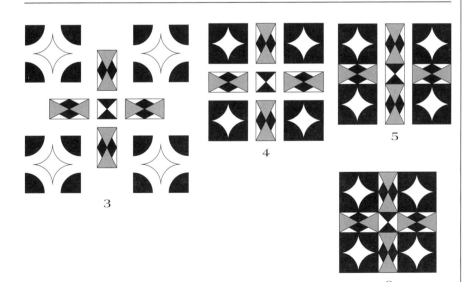

Area features exhibit buildings, mills, and displays of early industries. Early American furnishings are showcased in the Henry Francis du Pont Winterthur Museum near Wilmington. The Historical Society of Delaware makes use of Wilmington's Old Town Hall with exhibits and displays. It is for these reasons and more that historical and cultural attractions draw visitors from across the nation.

- The peach blossom is the state flower. Usually the peach tree is in full bloom before the leaves come out. They are believed to have come from China and seldom live longer than thirty years.

- The American holly is the best known of the native hollies. This is a bushy tree that prefers moist soil and grows along river bottoms. It reaches its best growth in the southeast. This holly has a heavy spiny evergreen leaf and smooth gray bark. There are male and female plants, and the bright red berries occur only on the female tree. These berries are a favorite food of songbirds.

- Blue hen chicken, the state bird, lives only in history in the form of a legend from the Revolutionary War. Soldiers owned fighting cocks, offspring of hens of a bluish color. These birds gained fame for their gameness and bravery and the men of the regiment were so courageous that they were nicknamed the "Blue Hen Chickens."

Delaware pattern – page 115

23

FLORIDA
The Sunshine
State

Florida was the 27th state admitted to the United States in 1845. Horticultural experiments with oranges and grapefruits in the 1890's helped make citrus fruit farming an important industry in this state. Winter Haven is noted for its bountiful citrus groves and an outlying area of about one hundred lakes. The first earth satellite was launched from Cape Canaveral in 1958, and in 1961 the first U.S. manned space flight was launched. Cape Canaveral was renamed Cape Kennedy, and in 1969 Apollo 11 was launched and made history by being the first spacecraft to land men on the moon. This state is surrounded by water to the east, south, and west. There are over 30,000 shallow lakes throughout the state, with Okeechobee being by far the largest. There are more kinds of fish in Florida waters than in any other part of the world. Most of southern Florida is made up of the Big Cypress swamp and the grassy marsh-

FLORIDA

This unusual block is named "Palm Leaf," and was chosen because the palm is the state tree.

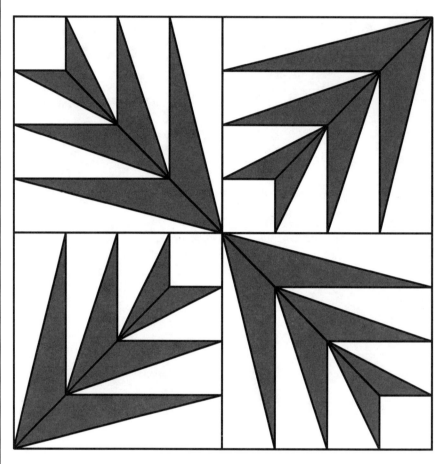

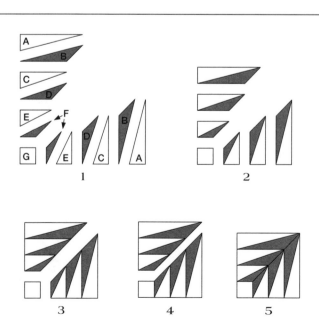

QUILT TOP

Because Florida has a very tropical ambiance this pattern is a great choice. Placing the "Palm Leaf" blocks side by side and top to bottom will give you this quilt top arrangement.

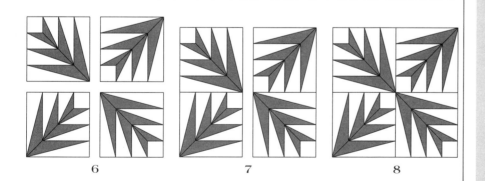

6   7   8

ASSEMBLY

Begin by laying out the pieces for each quarter of this block in this arrangement (1). Sew A to B, C to D, and E to F as shown for each quarter (2). Then attach these pieced segments together (3). Sew the G square to one of these pieced segments (4) and to finish the quarter sew these pieced segments together (5). Arrange these pieced squares as shown (6). Sew two of these squares together (7), and to complete the block sew these two strips together (8).

es of the Everglades. Spanning 128 miles, the Overseas Highway links the mainland with Key West. Miami and Miami Beach is a world class resort city featuring a tropical climate, white sand beaches, and luxurious hotels. *The* tourist attraction in this state has to be Orlando. Walt Disney World, Universal Studios, and Sea World sprawl around the Orlando area. These world-famous amusement and recreational centers keep the all-important tourist trade flourishing all year.

■ The mockingbird is the state bird. This bird builds a bulky nest of twigs, strings, and rags and prefers to place it in shrubs and thickets close to houses.

■ The orange blossom grows on a low-branching evergreen tree. This tree seldom grows over thirty feet tall and requires a warm climate. The blossoms, often appearing along with mature fruit, have waxy white petals and a strong fragrance. The orange tree is originally from Asia, and wild ones now found in Florida are descendants of trees brought in by early Spanish explorers.

■ The palm is a group of trees quite different from most other trees. They are more directly related to lilies, bananas, and bamboo than to ordinary trees like oaks and maples. The sabal palm, this state's tree, has a cluster of large, fan-shaped leaves topping a thick trunk that grows 20 to 30 feet tall.

Florida pattern – page 116

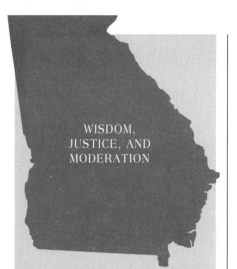

GEORGIA
Empire State of the South

Georgia was the 4th state admitted to the United States in 1789. Swimming, sunning, and shelling are favorite pastimes on the Atlantic coast and golden islands of this southern state. Famous for historic districts and restored antebellum homes, Georgia is rich in history and southern culture. The Antebellum Trail takes you to gracious and grand southern mansions in areas brimming with Victorian history. Savanna has restored the City Market in the center of its historic district. Here artists and craftspeople demonstrate their specialties in open lofts and sell their works. The coastal communities specialize in boating and salt-water fishing. The Masters Golf Tournament draws many tourists each April in Augusta. A prized fruit crop is celebrated in the 10-day Georgia Peach Festival in Peach County. The northern Georgia Mountains provide spectacular scenery and vivid fall colors. The Appalachian Trail begins in this rugged area of the state. The Chattooga Wild and

GEORGIA

This block is named "Georgia" and is easy to assemble.

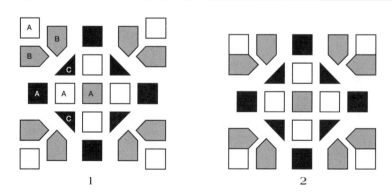

1   2

ASSEMBLY

Begin by laying out all the pieces in this arrangement (1). Attach A squares to B pieces (2). Then sew the remaining B pieces to these pieced segments (3). Attach triangles C to these pieced segments to make 4 pieced squares (4). Make 3 strips of the A blocks as shown (5). Sew these together to make three strips (6) and then sew these strips together to finish this block (7).

QUILT TOP

Place the "Georgia" blocks side by side and top to bottom to get this quilt top arrangement. When the corners of the blocks are joined an exciting secondary design is formed.

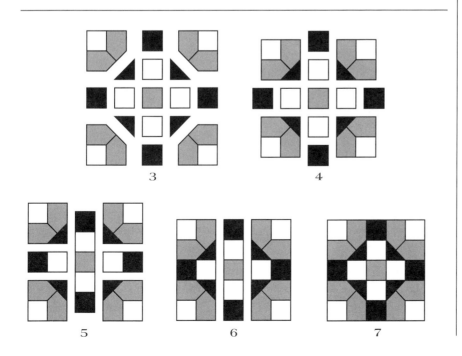

3   4

5   6   7

Georgia pattern – page 117

Scenic River with breathtaking woodlands and thrilling rapids provides the perfect environment for hikers, campers, and white-water rafters. Atlanta is one of the largest air transportation centers in the world and a top convention and tourism site in North America. The Atlanta Memorial Arts Center, a thirteen million dollar project, houses the Atlanta Ballet, Atlanta Opera, Atlanta Repertory Theater Company, Atlanta Symphony Orchestra, Atlanta School of Art, and High Museum of Art. The Atlanta Braves, Zoo Atlanta, Atlanta Cyclorama, Rhodes Memorial Hall, Atlanta Botanical Garden, the Carter Presidential Center, and many more tourist attractions and events call Atlanta their home.

■ Having a song that sounds much like the mockingbird, the brown thrasher is the state bird. Except when singing, this bird spends much of its time on the ground hunting insects.

■ The state flower is the Cherokee rose. Now a native wild rose, it was originally brought here from China. It is an evergreen rose with fragrant white flowers that bloom in the spring.

■ The live oak tree is the symbol of the south. It is a low-spreading tree often covered with Spanish moss. Its leaf is very different from the rest of the oak family. It is oval and blunt-tipped, leathery dark green, and remains on the tree throughout the year. The acorns are small and edible, and the wood is prized for furniture building.

HAWAII
The Aloha State

Hawaii was the 50th state admitted to the United States in 1959. Polynesians center their daily lives and religion on the wondrous natural beauties and sights found in this exotic state. Kauai, Oahu, Molokai, Lanai, Maui, and Hawaii are the islands that make up this state and each has a special attraction all its own. Oahu has the Polynesian Cultural Center that highlights the history and lifestyles found here. The somber U.S.S. Arizona Memorial is in the Pearl Harbor Bay of Oahu. Maui features Iao Needle, a 1,200 foot tall cinder cone in the Iao Valley State Park. Kauai is Hawaii's oldest principal island. It is called the Garden Island and is the home of the National Tropical Botanical Gardens. Lanai, the private island, gives a total sense of seclusion and privacy on a tropical island paradise. Molokai is the friendly island, with the quiet Kamakou Preserve, a tropical rain forest filled with rare birds and

HAWAII

The traditional quilt for Hawaii is an appliqué design, but in my research for this book I came across this patchwork block. It is named "Hawaii" and requires close attention to detail as you assemble it.

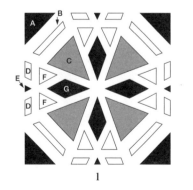

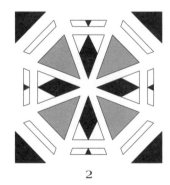

ASSEMBLY

Begin by laying out all the pieces in this arrangement (1). Attach triangles F to polygons G and sew pieces D to triangles E (2). Attach these two pieced segments together as shown (3). Sew pieces A, B, and C together (4). Attach these pieced segments together to make these 4 pieced portions (5). Sew these together to make two sections (6) and then sew these two together to finish this block (7).

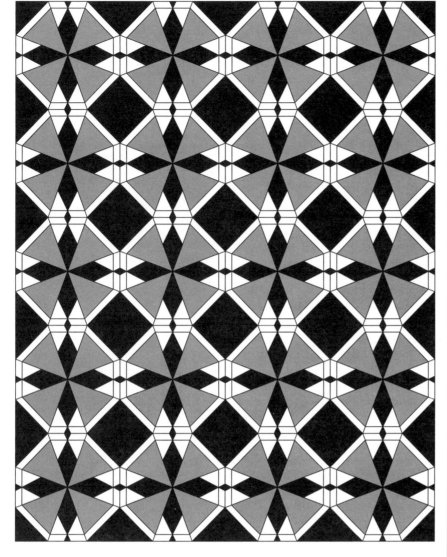

QUILT TOP

Place the "Hawaii" blocks side by side and top to bottom to get this quilt top arrangement.

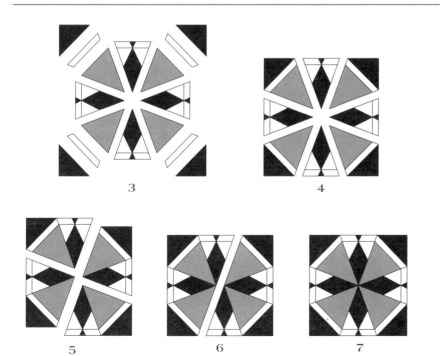

3   4

5   6   7

lush plant life. Hawaii is the largest island in the state, and was formed by five volcanoes. Two of those volcanoes are still active, Mauna Loa and Kilauea in the Hawaii Volcanoes National Park. Compared to other island crafts, quiltmaking is a relatively young art that came to the islands with missionaries in the early 1800's. Thousands of hours go into making an appliquéd Hawaiian quilt called a *kapa lau*. While no one knows the exact origin of this style of quilt, one story is that a native woman was working on a New England patchwork quilt under the shade of a ulu tree. The shadows cast by the spiky leaves inspired her to transfer the pattern to cloth. Cut like paper snowflakes, these designs are artistic interpretations of trees, fruits, ferns, or flowers.

- The state bird is the nene (Hawaiian goose). It is a close relative of the Canadian goose. It had become so endangered that it was put on the state "protected" list in 1949. Today its numbers are coming back and they can be found roaming wild in parts of Maui and Hawaii.

- The state flower is the yellow hibiscus. Thousands of types of this flower flourish in Hawaii.

- Kukui, also called the candlenut tree, is the state tree. It is a large tree that bears nuts containing white oily kernels formerly used for light. For this reason it is considered to be a symbol of enlightenment.

Hawaii pattern – page 118

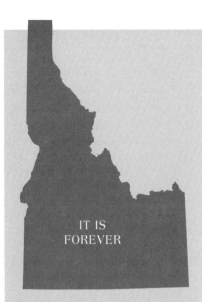

IDAHO
The Gem
State

Idaho was the 43rd state admitted to the United States in 1890. Gold was discovered in this mineral rich state in the 1860's and prospectors poured in. Towns grew overnight and when the mines played out, ghost towns were left. Cattlemen had moved to Idaho from California and Texas to feed the miners. As a result, cattle ranching grew as an industry as Idaho became an important supplier for the rest of the nation. Agriculture is this state's leading industry, and as you might guess the top crop is the potato. Natural wonders abound in this state and draw thousands of tourists and sightseers every year. Sun Valley is a popular ski resort, and with the numerous other ski resorts in this rugged Rocky Mountain state this is a skier's paradise. The deepest canyon in the nation, Hell's Canyon, is in this state on the Snake River. It is deeper than the Grand Canyon and a popular rafting site.

IDAHO

The "Idaho" block is a pattern that requires attention to detail as you assemble it.

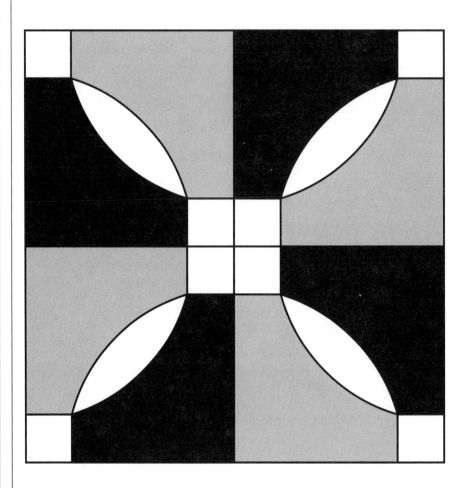

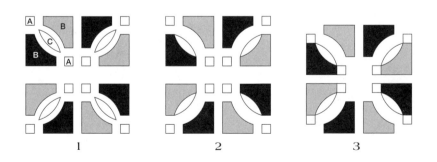

ASSEMBLY

Begin by laying out all the pieces in this arrangement (1). Sew pieces C to B (2) and then sew squares A to this pieced section (3). Sew the remaining B pieces to this pieced section to form 4 squares (4). Sew these squares into 2 strips (5), and to finish the block sew these 2 strips together (6).

QUILT TOP

Placing the "Idaho" blocks side by side and top to bottom will result in this quilt top. This will form a truly unique and interesting design. You can do dramatic things with this pattern by using different materials for the B pattern pieces.

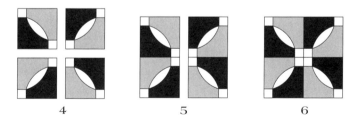

4   5   6

Shoshone Falls on the same river falls a distance greater than that of Niagara Falls. A small part of Yellowstone National Park is in this state. A truly unique area, Craters of the Moon National Monument, is found in southern Idaho. It is a region of volcanic cones, craters, caves, lava flows, and natural bridges that continually amazes tourists. A wealth of underground caverns, weird rock formations, mining ghost towns, waterfalls, forests, and parklands make this state a most popular tourist attraction.

- The western bluebird is about seven inches long with an azure blue coat and blue vest with white underfeathers. These beautiful birds build their nest in a hollow tree or crevice.

- The Syringa, a variety of the mock orange, is the state flower. The blossoms have four white petals and grow in clusters on a branching shrub. This variety grows up to twelve feet tall. After the flower petals fall away, seeds form, and when they are released the dry seed containers look like little brown flowers.

- The state tree is the western white pine. The largest remaining volume of this timber in the nation is found here in Idaho. This tree has many fine qualities like the straight grain and the soft even texture of the wood that make it a popular lumber.

Idaho pattern – page 120

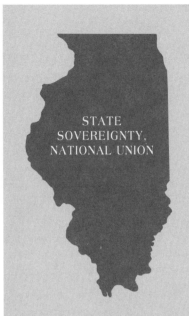

ILLINOIS
The Land
of Lincoln

Illinois was the 21st state admitted to the United States in 1818. Chicago on the southwest shore of Lake Michigan is the nation's third largest city. Doing things in a big way is traditional with this city. It produces more cookies, candy, soap, radios, televisions, paint, and machine tools than any other area of the country. It features one of the world's most beautiful lakefronts and has the world's tallest building, largest grain market, and busiest airport. The Museum of Science and Industry here hosts more than three million visitors each year. Chicago's tradition of architectural dominance began after the Great Chicago Fire of 1871 destroyed much of the city. The most notable development of the resulting Chicago School of architecture was the skyscraper. In the Civic Center Plaza is perhaps the most recognizable

ILLINOIS

The "Illinois" block is a clever design that is fairly easy to assemble.

ASSEMBLY

Begin by laying out all the pieces in this arrangement (1). Sew triangles A together and triangles B to C and triangles B to center square D to form these blocks (2). Then attach these pieced blocks together to form these 9 squares (3). Sew the resulting squares into 3 strips (4) and sew the strips together to finish the block (5).

QUILT TOP

Place the "Illinois" blocks side by side and top to bottom to form this design. When sewn together in this manner it forms a second arrangement that is reminiscent of the flying geese pattern.

3

4

5

piece of art associated with Chicago, the five story steel sculpture by Pablo Picasso. The Mississippi River forms the entire western border of this Midwestern state and makes river industries very important here. Abraham Lincoln won national fame in Illinois during his debates with Stephen Douglas. Today you may visit the white frame house where Lincoln lived, preserved as a national historic site. The Shawnee National Forest in Southern Illinois is a wonder-filled area of valleys, rocky bluffs, and natural springs. Hiking, bike-riding, camping, and picnicking are popular here most of the year. Hundreds of thousands of Canadian Geese spend the winter at sanctuaries in Southern Illinois and one of the largest feeding and resting grounds for wild ducks in North America is the Illinois River valley.

■ The cardinal is the state bird. Indiana, Kentucky, North Carolina, Ohio, Virginia, and West Virginia also claim this popular bird.

■ Rhode Island, Wisconsin, and New Jersey share the violet family of flowers with Illinois as their state flower.

■ The white oak is the state tree for illinois, Maryland, and Connecticut.

Illinois pattern – page 121

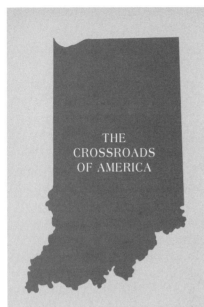

INDIANA
The Hoosier State

Indiana was the 19th state admitted to the United States in 1816. This state is the proud home of many celebrities – Polly Bergen, Bill Blass, James Dean, Michael Jackson and family, David Letterman, Karl Malden, Steve McQueen, Betsy Palmer, Jane Pauley, and Red Skelton just to name a few. In its capital, the Indianapolis 500 automobile race is a worldwide tourist attraction that takes place every year during Memorial Day weekend. This state is also internationally known for the 32 covered bridges found here. Turkey Run, Shades, and Raccoon Lake State Parks, the milltowns of Bridgeton and Mansfield, and the county seat of Rockville host a unique celebration known as the Annual Covered Bridge Festival. The Old Bag Factory in Goshen has become a renovated marketplace for artists and craftspersons featuring pot-

INDIANA

As I began drafting this block called "Indiana" it quickly became apparent that it was going to be quite a challenge to assemble, but because I wanted a block with the state name here it is.

ASSEMBLY

Begin by laying out all the pieces in this arrangement (1). Sew D pieces to center piece E (2). Then attach C pieces to this pieced section to make the center square (3). Sew pieces B to A (4) and attach remaining B pieces to AB section to complete corners (5). To finish the block, sew the corner sections to the center pieced block (6).

QUILT TOP

This unusual and very bold design is the result of placing the "Indiana" blocks side by side and top to bottom. I prefer blocks that, when assembled, combine to make a secondary design, and this is a good example.

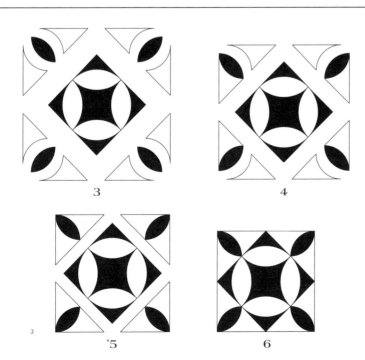

3   4

'5   6

tery, sculpture, stained glass, fine custom-made quilts, and more. Brown County to the south draws many artists to the Brown County Art Galleries in Nashville. This area highlights doll and pottery making, weaving, woodworking, and many more traditional and unusual arts and crafts. Visiting the Amish country of northern Indiana will give you a chance to learn about the "plain" people and their unique way of life. The Menno-Hof Mennonite-Amish Visitors Center and Amish Acres in Nappanee are two places that showcase this lifestyle.

■ This Midwestern state has the bright red cardinal as its state bird. Because this bird is so colorful and quite common throughout the eastern half of the United States, it is the bird of choice for several states. The male is totally red except for a distinctive black mask from his eye to his bill and below. He has a red beak and unique red crest on the top of his scarlet head.

■ The Indiana state flower is the showy peony. Its blossom is usually white, pink, red, or combinations of these colors in hybrid versions. The blossom is large, and shows up well on its dark green bushy leaves and stems.

■ Indiana, often referred to as the Hoosier state, has the tulip tree or yellow poplar as its state tree. This tree has creamy-yellow wood with a grayish, thick and ridged bark. It is a cousin of the magnolia tree.

Indiana pattern – page 122

IOWA
The Hawkeye
State

Iowa was the 29th state admitted to the United States in 1846. This is an important agricultural state with the State Fair as one of the most important annual events. It is a celebration featuring many farming prizes, accomplishments, and innovations. Iowa is second only to California in providing food for the nation. The majority of this state's area is farmland with a fifth of its population living on farms. The Mississippi River forms the eastern border and the Missouri River forms the western border of this Midwestern state. All the rivers that stream through this state flow into the Mississippi. Prehistoric Indians built earthen mounds in many recognizable animal shapes in northeastern Iowa. Effigy Mounds National Monument was established here in 1949 to protect and preserve these historic sites. Josiah Grinnell left New York in 1854, traveled to Iowa, and founded the city of Grinnell after the famous advice he was given by Horace Greeley: "Go west, young man, go west and

IOWA

This quilt block is named "Iowa Star." It is a high-contrast design that is fairly simple to piece.

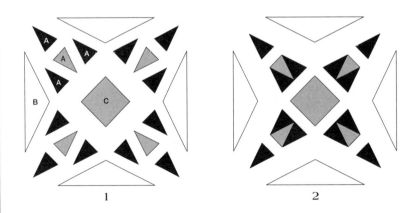

ASSEMBLY

Begin by laying out all the pieces in this arrangement (1). Sew A triangles together as shown (2). Then join the remaining A triangle to these pieced segments (3). Piece triangles B to two of these pieced segments. Attach the remaining pieced triangles to the center square C (4). Finish the block by sewing these segments together as shown (5).

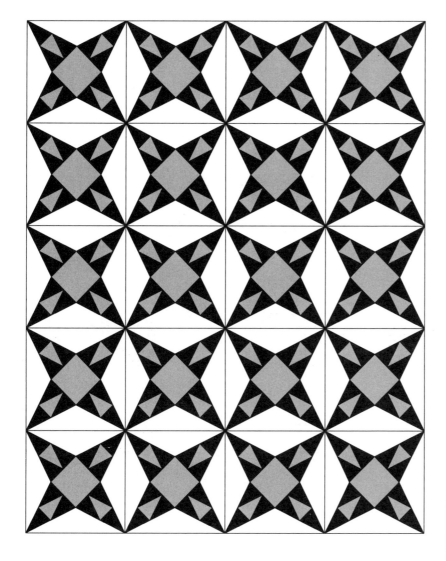

QUILT TOP

The quilt top is the result of placing the "Iowa Star" blocks side by side and top to bottom. It is a very bold design and a desirable quilt pattern.

3

4

5

grow up with the country." Tourism is a growing industry here. The many lakes and streams offer fishing and watersports. Hunting and other outdoor sports are important tourist attractions in the winter as well as summer. Craftspeople of the state are showcased in Amana Colonies, an area that honors its early inhabitants. Weavers, spinners, and quilters perform their trade in these preserved settlements for tourists to enjoy and purchase.

■ Ranging in color from dark to pale pink and even white, the wild rose is Iowa's state flower. After the petals fall from this flower bright red berries form and attract birds throughout the winter. The thorns of this plant protect it from foraging animals and aid in stabilizing it as it grows and climbs

■ The oak tree is the state tree. Considered a symbol of strength, this family of trees usually bears a nut called an acorn. It has a larger rough surfaced cap that holds a smooth, sometimes pointed nut within. Indians of the past used these as food and today they are an important food source for wildlife. It produces the most important hardwood timber, but as a slow-growing tree it needs to be carefully forested.

■ The Eastern goldfinch is the Iowa state bird.

Iowa pattern – page 124

KANSAS

This quilt block is named "Kansas Star." Only two pieces make up this block and yet it looks very involved. Based on a Nine-Patch arrangement, it is an easy block to assemble.

KANSAS
The Sunflower State

Kansas was the 34th state admitted to the United States in 1861. The Flint Hills is the only extensive unplowed tract of true prairie remaining in the nation. In Logan and Grove counties chalkbeds are some of the world's most extensive pre-historic fossil specimens. With many federal reservoirs, lakes, and wildlife areas sportsmen come here to hunt a wide spectrum of game. In the 1870's Mennonites from Russia brought a new variety of winter wheat that boosted this state's crop production. Today Kansas farmers are the leading producers of wheat in the United States. This state's history is also closely tied to the beef industry. Kansas honors its longhorn heritage during the Dodge City Days celebration. It is an event featuring a five-day PRCA rodeo, the fourth largest in the nation. Dodge City gained fame in the late 1800's as the world's largest cattle market. The Chisholm Trail funneled great herds of cattle here along with the rugged men that drove them. Booming cow towns became dangerously unlawful and

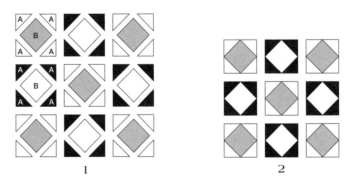

1   2

ASSEMBLY

Begin by laying out all the pieces in this arrangement (1). Sew A triangles to B squares to make pieced squares (2). Join these squares into three strips (3). To complete the block sew the strips together (4).

QUILT TOP

Place the "Kansas Star" blocks side by side and top to bottom. This quilt top features a definite crosshatch design that makes good use of many types of material.

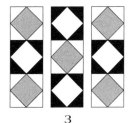

3

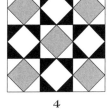

4

soon drew such famous lawmen as Wyatt Earp, Bat Masterson, and Wild Bill Hickok. Swedish and German immigrants settling in Lindsborg began the tradition of the Messiah Festival of Music and Art presented each spring. Each year this religious celebration draws thousands of tourists and is a nationally broadcast radio and television program. With frontier forts, a Pony Express station, and early cow towns preserved for all to see, this is a state that treasures its colorful past and the adventure and excitement of the American West.

■ The wild native sunflower, the state's flower, has a sunburst of golden ray petals that surround hundreds of little brown seed-bearing disk flowers in its center. It is a tall, hardy perennial, and its daisy-like blooms are now very popular in decorating. These yellow beauties bloom from July through October and are an excellent choice for the back of wide borders when used as an ornamental.

■ Wyoming and Nebraska share the cottonwood with Kansas as a state tree.

■ The western meadowlark is the state bird as it is with Nebraska, Montana, North Dakota, Oregon, and Wyoming.

Kansas pattern – page 126

KENTUCKY

This quilt block is named "Kentucky Crossroad" and has a definite "X" design with a Nine-Patch in the center.

KENTUCKY
The Bluegrass State

Kentucky was the 15th state admitted to the United States in 1792. This state has long been associated with horse racing and hosts the Kentucky Derby, the first race in the Triple Crown, at Churchill Downs in Louisville each spring. Over thirty horse farms in the Lexington area are open to the public. The state of Kentucky links two major features of the nation, the Appalachian Mountains to the east and the Mississippi River to the west. The Ohio River forms the northern border of the state. Land Between the Lakes is a federal park that lies between the man-made Kentucky Lake and Lake Barkley in Western Kentucky. This natural area provides many hunting and recreational activities. Tourists visit the natural wonders of the Cumberland Gap and Mammoth Cave no matter the season. Phyllis George Brown began promoting the craftspeople of this state and helped initiate a movement that helped to make country-style handcrafts popular. Paducah, a western town on

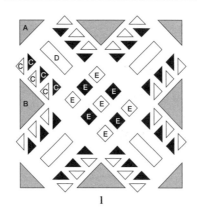

1

2

ASSEMBLY

Begin by laying out all the pieces in this arrangement (1). Attach C triangles together to form strips and sew E squares into 3 strips (2). Sew these pieced strips into blocks (3) then sew 3 of these pieced blocks to make a diagonal strip. Attach A and B triangles to these pieced sections (4). To complete the block add the pieced triangles to the center pieced diagonal strip (5).

QUILT TOP

Place the "Kentucky Crossroads" blocks side by side and top to bottom to form this arrangement. This results in a traditional quilt top featuring a center Nine-Patch.

3

4

5

the Ohio River is home to the American Quilter's Society, founded by Meredith and Bill Schroeder. The annual AQS Quilt Show and Contest is held here each April with participants from all over the United States and abroad. It draws the top professionals in the quilting industry and is a must to attend for quilting enthusiasts. The Museum of the American Quilter's Society is located in downtown Paducah, just a block from the Ohio riverfront. It features seminars, lectures, and demonstrations as well as gallery shows that are presented throughout the year. All these quilting activities have given Paducah the nickname "Quilt City U.S.A."

■ The Kentucky state flower is the goldenrod, an excellent choice for ornamental borders or rock gardens. It is a very hardy perennial with golden plumes of tiny clustered flowers. It is also the state flower for Nebraska.

■ Tulip poplar is Kentucky's state tree along with neighboring Tennessee and Indiana. This tree features a blossom that blends from green to a peculiar orange that opens in May and June. As it is a distant cousin of the magnolia, the center develops a fruit shaped like a cone composed of small winged seeds.

■ There are very few red birds and the Kentucky state bird, the cardinal, is the most distinctive one. It is also the state bird for Illinois, Indiana, North Carolina, Ohio, Virginia, and West Virginia.

Kentucky pattern – page 127

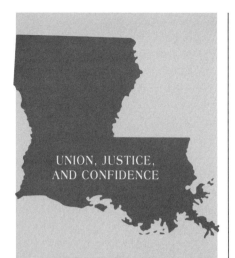

LOUISIANA
The Pelican State

Louisiana was the 18th state admitted to the United States in 1812. It has a general coastline of almost 400 miles along the Gulf. But the low marshy area found here and the bays, offshore islands, and emptying river deltas gives this state a tidal shoreline of almost 8,000 miles. Because rich soil deposits from southbound rivers are found here agriculture is an important industry. Rice is the most important crop closely followed by sugar cane. It also is a leading provider of oil and natural gas. The mighty Mississippi River marks the major portion of this state's eastern border. It then cuts through the state to empty into the Gulf of Mexico through the Mississippi Delta at New Orleans. This city is the chief tourist attraction with its French and Spanish quarters and the rowdy and colorful Mardi Gras celebration held each year. New Orleans is a wonderful blend of old and new. The new Superdome is as much a recognized landmark as is the

LOUISIANA

This quilt block is named "Louisiana." This is a bold, simple design that is very easy to assemble.

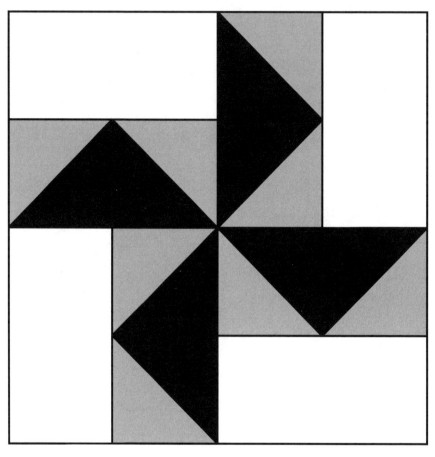

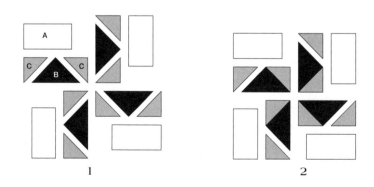

ASSEMBLY

Begin by laying out all the pieces in this arrangement (1). Attach C triangles to B (2) and then attach remaining C triangles to this BC section (3). Sew A rectangles to pieced BC sections to form 4 squares (4). Sew these pieced squares together to form 2 strips (5). To complete this simple block sew these 2 strips together (6).

QUILT TOP

Placing the "Louisiana" blocks side by side and top to bottom will result in this interesting design featuring the center pinwheels.

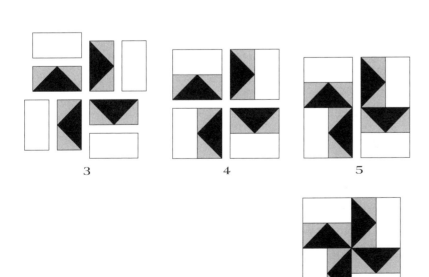

3   4   5

6

Historic St. Louis Cathedral. Jazz was developed in the early 1900's in the bars and nightclubs of the French Quarter. Today New Orleans style jazz is still performed throughout the city and is a specialty at Preservation Hall. All these tourist attractions blend together to give New Orleans the title of America's Most Interesting City.

- The magnolia is the state flower as it is in the neighboring state of Mississippi.

- The bald cypress is a tall pyramidal tree that grows best in moist or wet soils. This makes the marshes and swamp lands of Louisiana the perfect home for this state tree. In the swamps conical "knees" grow up above the water line from the roots of this tree to provide air for submerged parts. It is a deciduous tree even though it is in the pine family, and its hemlock-like leaves are tiny and feathery. The durable wood this tree provides is resistant to rotting. This feature makes it very popular for construction and posts. Where winters are mild the bald cypress is used as an ornamental.

- Since the coastline is so vast the Eastern brown pelican seems a good choice for the state bird. A large water bird, its wing span is over six feet. It is almost always silent and, while clumsy when walking, is most graceful in flight with a very rhythmic wing beat.

Louisiana pattern – page 128

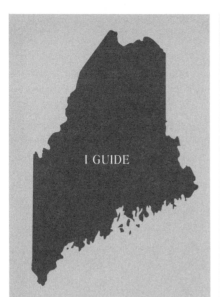

MAINE
The Pine Tree State

Maine was the 23rd state admitted to the United States in 1820. This state's breathtaking beauty is due to the spectacular White Mountains, the quiet forests, and picturesque farmland of the Eastern New England Upland and over 3,500 miles of scenic ocean shores of the Coastal Lowlands. The Kennebec and Moose River valleys are found in the heart of the state. They offer whitewater rafting, hiking, camping and an abundance of other outdoor summer and winter sports and activities. Shipbuilding was Maine's first industry due partly to the availability of lumber from vast forest areas. Today paper production from these forests is the most important industry in the state. Fish and shellfish also provide a lucrative and valued income with the annual lobster catch larger than any other state. Almost every coastal harbor, no matter how small, has a fleet of fishing boats. A popu-

MAINE

This quilt block is named "Maine." This design is a definite challenge to assemble, so take your time and mark your seam allowances, especially on the curved pieces.

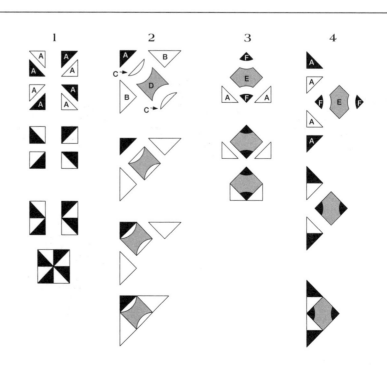

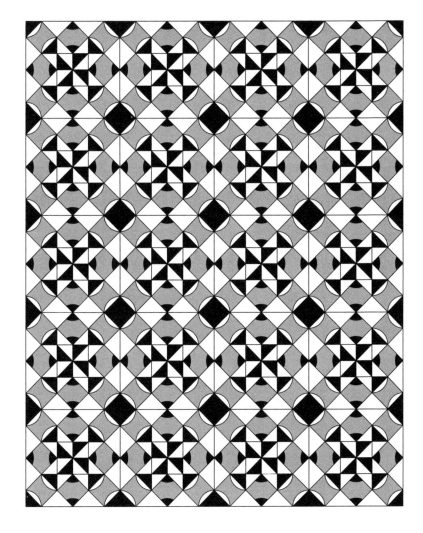

QUILT TOP

Place the "Maine" blocks side by side and top to bottom to achieve this design. It is a time-consuming block to piece, but it makes a very handsome quilt top.

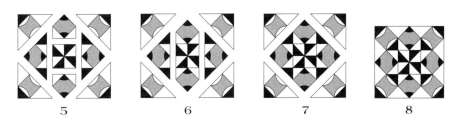

ASSEMBLY

Begin by assembling the center pinwheel. Lay out pattern pieces A as shown and assemble the center block by sewing A triangles together, then sewing these pieced squares into two strips. Finish the center square by sewing these two strips together (1). Next assemble each of the 4 corners. Lay out pattern pieces A, B, C, and D. Attach C to D and then sew A and B triangles to this pieced square (2). Assemble the AEF section as shown (3). And then assemble the next AEF section (4). Lay out all of these pieced sections as shown in (5). Assemble the center square by attaching the top and bottom AEF sections to the center A pinwheel (6). Then attach AEF pieced triangles to this resulting section (7). Finish (at last!) by sewing the corner ABCD triangles to the center block (8).

lar annual event in this ruggedly scenic state is the Maine Seafoods Festival held in Rockland during the first week in August. Cultural events, recreational opportunities, unique antique shops, and talented craftspeople are contributing factors that draw tourists to the quaint New England villages that are found throughout the state.

■ Maine has an unusual state flower. It is the white pinecone and tassel from the state tree, the white pine. This tree is a fast-growing evergreen that sometimes reaches a height of 200 feet. The needles are three-sided, bluish green, three to five inches long and grow in sets of five. They group along a branch end and form a tassel. Strong winds will not harm these trees and the sound it makes passing through the boughs is unique to long-needled pines. Two cones are found on this tree. The pollen bearing cone is small and falls off the tips of the branches in a few weeks. The seed-bearing cone begins in the green unripe stage and develops to the familiar woody brown cone holding winged seeds.

■ The chickadee is the state bird of Maine and Massachusetts.

Maine pattern – page 129

MARYLAND

This quilt block is named "Maryland Beauty." It is vaguely reminiscent of the ocean waves pattern.

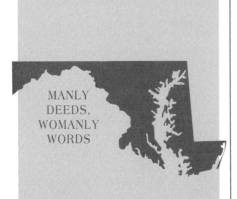
MARYLAND
The Old Line State

Maryland was the 7th state admitted to the United States in 1788. This is a state of strong historical traditions. Annapolis was the nation's capital from 1783 to 1784 and is home to the U.S. Naval Academy. In 1791 the state ceded the District of Columbia to the Congress of the United States for the capital of the nation. The Star Spangled Banner was written by Francis Scott Key while watching the battle at Fort McHenry during the war of 1812. The Tom Thumb, the first American coal-burning steam locomotive, was developed by the Baltimore and Ohio Railroad. Chesapeake Bay almost divides the state into two parts. The Chesapeake and Delaware Canal was completed in 1829 to connect the Chesapeake Bay to the Delaware River. Stretching across the western portion of the state, the Allegheny, Appalachian, and Blue Ridge Mountains supply a bounty of natural beauty. The Sport of Kings, horse racing, holds one

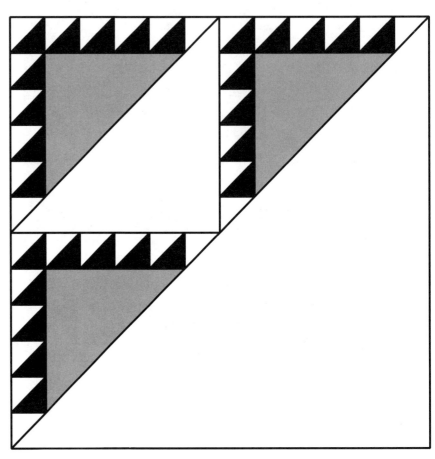

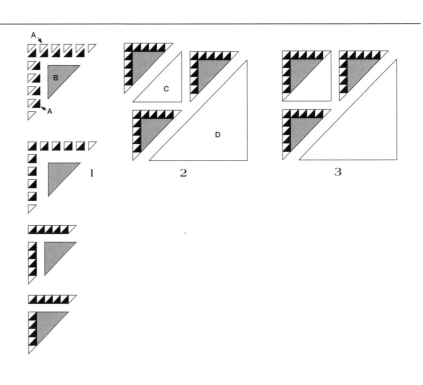

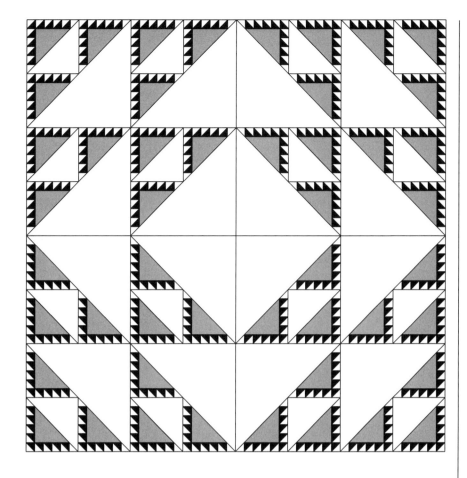

QUILT TOP

Place 4 of the Maryland Beauty blocks side by side and top to bottom. Then reverse this arrangement to make the top half of the quilt. Mirror the arrangement of this top half to get this resulting quilt top arrangement.

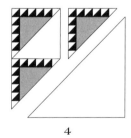
4

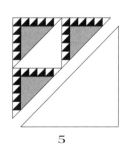
5

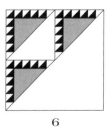
6

ASSEMBLY PAGE

Begin by assembling each pieced triangle. Sew small A triangles together and sew these pieced squares into strips as shown. Then attach these strips to triangle B. Do this for each of 3 pieced triangles (1). Lay out the rest of the block as shown (2). Attach C triangle to pieced triangle AB (3). Then attach the next pieced triangle AB to this pieced section (4). Complete this half of the block by attaching the remaining pieced triangle (5). Finish the block by sewing largest triangle D to this pieced triangle ABC (6).

of its most famous events in Baltimore. Part of the Triple Crown, the Preakness at Pimlico Race Track is an annual must for horse racing enthusiasts.

■ The stems of the daisy-like state flower, the black-eyed Susan, are covered with short bristles. They were originally western flowers, but now grow wherever there is a sunny field or roadside. The flowers are three inches across with golden-yellow petals surrounding a deep brown-purple center cone. As a point of interest it has 13 petals, symbolic of the number of original colonies. This flower is very showy and hardy, and as a result is becoming popular as an ornamental.

■ Found throughout New England, the white oak is the most common and best known of the oak family with the most recognizable leaf. In open areas this majestic tree develops a broad symmetrical crown. It is an outstanding lumber tree used for furniture, architecture, and boat building. However, it is very slow growing and prefers rich soil. To be more specific, the state tree is the Wye Oak at Wye Mills on Maryland's eastern shore. It is over 400 years old, more than 100 feet tall, with a spread of 165 feet, and is one of the largest in the world.

■ It is only natural that the Baltimore oriole is the state bird. It was named in honor of Lord Baltimore's colors of black and yellow. The male has brilliant flame-orange plumage with a black head, neck, upper back, and throat. They construct a hanging pouch-shaped nest of twine and fiber with a lining of hair.

Maryland pattern – page 130

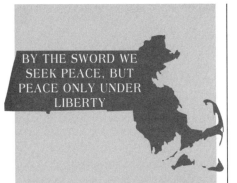

MASSACHUSETTS The Bay State

Massachusetts was the 6th state admitted to the United States in 1788. Pilgrims' landing at Plymouth, Harvard's founding in 1636, the Boston Tea Party, the beginning of the Revolutionary War, and industrial developments and inventions are only part of what makes this state a cultural and historical center. Boston is this state's capital. It is a major seaport and airport terminal and educational center. The telephone was invented in this city by Alexander Graham Bell in 1876. Elias Howe invented the sewing machine after he had moved to Boston from Spencer to learn the machinist trade. While serving an apprenticeship in Cambridge he developed his invention, but it was only after a patent battle that he made a fortune from it. Cape Cod, Walden Pond, Plymouth Plantation, Old Sturbridge Village, and the Minute Man National Historical Park are some of this state's attractions. Tourists are drawn here by the historic landmarks, monuments, memorials, seashores, and villages that fill this small state.

MASSACHUSETTS

This quilt block is named "Massachusetts," and 129 mostly tiny pieces make up this block. As you may have guessed this is a bit of a challenge to piece, but an excellent choice to use up your small fabric scraps.

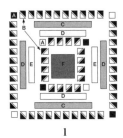

1

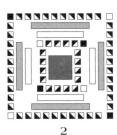

2

3

ASSEMBLY

Begin by laying out all the pieces in this arrangement (1). Sew all B triangles together (2) then sew these triangles and A squares into strips as shown (3). Attach the row of pieced segments to center square (4). Attach the next row of pieced segments (5). Attach E rectangles next (6), then attach light D rectangles (7). Attach medium-light D rectangles next (8) and then attach C rectangles (9). Next attach outer pieced row (10) and finish by sewing last pieced row to the block (11).

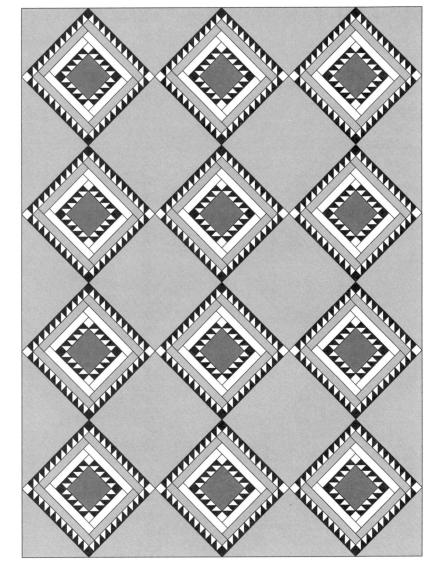

QUILT TOP

Place medium color 12" blocks between these "Massachusetts" blocks turned 45° on point to make this quilt top arrangement.

- Often blooming before winter snows have melted, this state's flower is the trailing arbutus, or mayflower. It a vigorous, low-growing, evergreen ground cover with oval dark green leaves. The blossoms are very fragrant and rose-pink paling to white as they mature.

- The state tree of Massachusetts, along with North Dakota, is the American elm.

- The state bird, the chickadee, is a chatty little bird that makes a call sounding much like his name. They are dark and light gray with a black cap, white cheeks, and a white bib. They seem to enjoy winter weather and are very acrobatic to the extent of hanging upside down or clinging sideways to a perch.

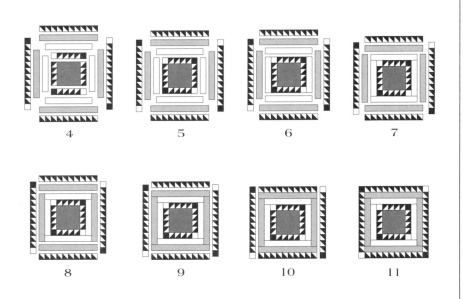

4 5 6 7

8 9 10 11

Massachusetts pattern – page 132

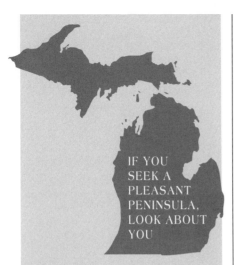

MICHIGAN
The Wolverine State

Michigan was the 26th state admitted to the United States in 1837. It is a leading agricultural state producing corn, beans, apples, cherries, and more. In 1896 Henry Ford built the first automobile in Detroit, beginning this city's long history of car manufacturing. Michigan is a leading producer of transportation equipment in the nation. This state has over 3,000 miles of shoreline with four Great Lakes (Erie, Michigan, Superior, and Huron) as boundaries. As you may expect tourism is an important and thriving business here. Hunting is a popular sport with the deer population over a million. Elk and moose also range in this rugged state. Kellogg Bird Sanctuary is a hundred-acre refuge for ducks, partridges, pheasants, and other wild birds on Gull Lake near Battle Creek. Some of the nation's finest collections of plants, shrubs, and trees are found at the Leila Arboretum in Battle Creek and Nichols Arboretum

MICHIGAN

This quilt block is named "Michigan Beauty." It is a simple, bold design that is both easy to cut out and easy to make.

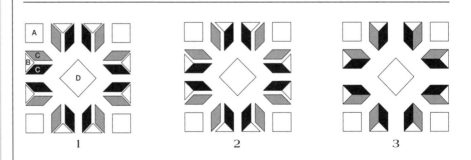

ASSEMBLY

Begin by laying out all the pieces in this arrangement (1). Attach B triangles to pattern C pieces (2). Then sew remaining C pieces to sections CB (3). Sew square A to pieced section BC (4) and then attach remaining pieced sections BC to this ABC section, completing the corners (5). Sew two opposite corner sections to center block D (6) and complete the block by attaching the remaining corners (7).

QUILT TOP

Place the "Michigan Beauty" blocks side by side and top to bottom to form this quilt top design.

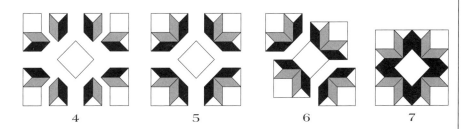

4   5   6   7

in Ann Arbor. Two opposite but unique attractions are Mackinac Island, a resort island where no automobiles are allowed, and the natural beauty of the colored cliffs of Pictured Rocks on Lake Superior. The many streams, lakes, springs, and waterfalls of this two peninsula state make up its natural scenic beauty. With all these outdoor wonders, both winter and summer sports and attractions keep tourists visiting here year round.

■ The apple blossom has a deep pink bud that opens to be a white flower streaked with pink. These blossoms are grouped on short twigs of the tree. Bees and other insects are attracted to these small flowers and carry pollen from flower to flower, aiding in fruit production. Because Michigan exports so many apples, it is only natural for the apple blossom to be the state flower.

■ White pine is the state tree. It is very hardy and valuable for timber. To keep a good supply of lumber for this state, foresters plant more trees than are harvested each year.

■ The robin arrives in early spring and begins making its bulky nest of twigs, mud, and grass. The eggs of this most common native bird are a lovely greenish-blue. Because a sharp image is visible only through the center of its eye, it has a strange habit of cocking its head to one side to look on the ground for food. Robins seldom eat seeds, preferring apples, grapes, cherries, or raisins as feeder food.

Michigan pattern – page 134

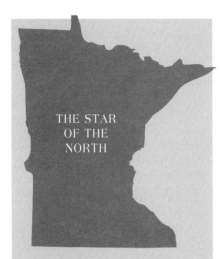

MINNESOTA
The Gopher State

Minnesota was the 32nd state admitted to the United States in 1858. The world-famous Mayo Clinic was built in Rochester in 1889. It is a state that produces much of the nation's wheat, flour, and dairy products. Long, frigid winters make winter carnivals and celebrations a welcome distraction from the harsh weather. St. Paul's Winter Carnival, snowmobile races in Alexandria, sled dog races in Ely, and the Red River Valley Winter Show in Crookston are just a few of these winter events. Legendary lumberjack Paul Bunyan and his blue ox Babe are remembered with statues in Bemidji. The state is blessed with many state and national parklands and forests. Thousands of lakes are found here, and Lake Superior forms the northeastern border. In the rugged Superior Upland you can walk across the mighty Mississippi River at its source. The high falls of the Pigeon River is a favorite tourist site,

MINNESOTA

This quilt block named "Minnesota," is a bold, easy-to-assemble pattern.

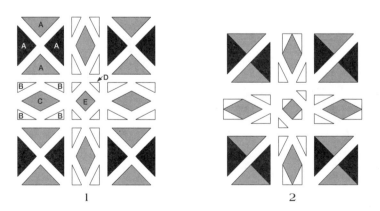

ASSEMBLY

Begin by laying out all the pieces in this arrangement (1). Attach the A triangles together, the B triangles to piece C, and D triangles to square E (2). Sew pieced A triangles together to make a pieced square and finish sewing B triangles to pieced BC section and D triangles to pieced DE section to make blocks as shown (3). Then sew these blocks together to form these 3 strips (4). To complete this block sew these strips together (5).

QUILT TOP

This Minnesota quilt block looks really simple. But because of the medium and dark arrangements of the A pattern triangles, when the blocks are placed side by side and top to bottom an unusual pattern develops.

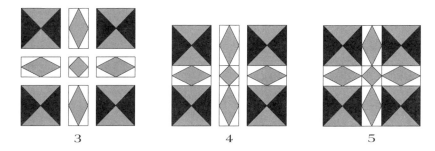

3   4   5

and one of the most beautiful waterfalls is Minnehaha Falls featured in the famous poem, "The Song of Hiawatha." For watersports as well as hunting, fishing, hiking, and camping, Minnesota is a popular tourist haven due to the sparkling springs, rivers, and lakes found here.

- The state flower is the showy lady's slipper. This large wild orchid has a bloom that is more than three inches long with a large petal that forms a pouch. Despite their exotic reputation, this wild species is remarkably tolerant and can withstand considerable neglect.

- Norway pine is the state tree. Minnesota's large scenic wilderness areas are covered with evergreen forests that abound with Norway, white, and jack pine trees.

- The state bird is the common loon. They nest in wooded lakes and make a remarkable, almost eerie, yodeling call. The male has a black dagger-like bill and a glossy dark green head. Their body is large and long with a short neck. The plumage is heavily checkered black and white fading to solid white underparts.

Minnesota pattern – page 135

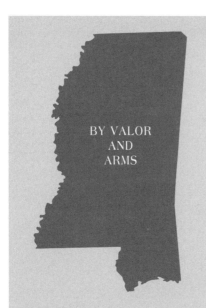

MISSISSIPPI
The Magnolia State

Mississippi was the 20th state admitted to the United States in 1817. Lumber from the Piney Woods of the East Gulf Coastal Plains region provides lumber and pine products from the loblolly, longleaf, and slash pines that grow there. Oil was discovered in 1939 at Tinsley and today this state is a leading producer of oil and natural gas. Cotton is Mississippi's most important agricultural product. The Delta and Pine Land Company Plantation is one of the largest cotton plantations in the world, covering 38,000 acres. As you might expect, centers for the fabric and clothing industry abound across this state. The nation's most important river, the Mississippi, forms the entire western border of this southern state. Many fine examples of antebellum homes are found in Biloxi, Natchez, Columbus, and Holly Springs. Confederate battlegrounds and monuments, and historic

MISSISSIPPI

This quilt block is named "Mississippi Star." It has a very bold four-point star featured in the center.

1   2

ASSEMBLY

Begin by laying out all the pieces in this arrangement (1). Sew B triangles together (2). Then sew these pieced triangles to square A (3). Attach C pieces to pieced AB triangles (4). Sew center pieces E together (5) and then sew triangle D to this center star (6). To complete the block sew the corner pieced sections to the center pieced section (7).

QUILT TOP

Place these blocks side by side and top to bottom to make this quilt top. It is a very bold design in which the corner squares of the blocks form large squares throughout the quilt top.

3

4

5

6

7

river and gulf harbors are only a part of the treasures that make this state rich in traditional southern culture.

■ The state flower and tree is the fragrant magnolia. The creamy white blossoms have six to twelve waxen petals. When the petals fall away the seed capsules form a composite fruit shaped like a cone. These large blossoms are emphasized by the dark green, glossy, leathery leaves that have a rusty-brown underside. These trees prefer rich, moist soil and grow well in swamps and river banks. This southern species is very popular as an ornamental but are not hardy to areas in the north.

■ Along with Texas, Tennessee, Florida, and Arkansas, Mississippi's state bird is the mockingbird.

Mississippi pattern – page 136

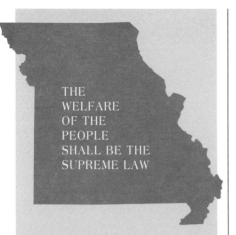

MISSOURI
The Show Me State

Missouri was the 24th state admitted to the United States in 1821. Mark Twain used this scenic state as a backdrop for the adventures of his most popular character, Tom Sawyer. Each year in Hannibal, Twain's hometown, the National Tom Sawyer Fence Painting Contest is held. In business for only 18 months in 1860 and 1861, the Pony Express began in St. Joseph, Missouri, and linked it to Sacramento, California. Livestock centers and corn and soybean production make this a leading agricultural state. St. Louis and Kansas City have chief U.S. air and rail terminals. With the Mississippi River as the eastern border, river traffic is equally important. All these transportation features make it only natural that manufacturing is a large income-producing resource. Missouri is a state that emphasizes handcraft skills and hands them down generation to generation. The success of Branson as a tourist center began by featuring handcrafts as well as performing arts. The

MISSOURI

This quilt block is named "Missouri Windmill." The unique center windmill is surrounded by two diagonal strips.

ASSEMBLY

Begin by laying out all the pieces in this arrangement (1). Sew D and E triangles together (2). Then sew these pieced sections together (3). Attach these pieced squares together (4) and then sew these two strips together to form the center windmill. Sew C triangles to windmill (5). Sew A triangles to B pieces (6), and to finish the block attach these corner pieces to the center section (7).

QUILT TOP

Placing these blocks side by side and top to bottom will result in this pattern – a very bold quilt top with the windmill pattern as a special feature.

4

5

6

7

Gateway Arch, Climatron at Missouri Botanical Gardens, and McDonnell Planetarium are only three of the attractions found in St. Louis. The Ozark Plateau in this state abounds with bubbling mineral and fresh-water springs. The Current River is one of Missouri's most scenic areas, with river sports of all kinds drawing tourists to this beautifully rugged and lush natural attraction.

- The state flower, hawthorn, is also called the "red haw" or "white haw." This small tree has many clusters of small white flowers on every twig that develops into bright red fruit. It may grow to a height of 30 feet and has many tiny branches and twigs armed with sharp spines nearly two inches long.

- Missouri's state tree, the flowering dogwood, is also Virginia's and North Carolina's state flower.

- The bluebird is Missouri's state bird. This native species is bright blue with a cinnamon colored breast. It is considered a symbol of happiness and makes its home throughout Missouri from early spring until late November.

Missouri pattern – page 137

MONTANA
The Treasure State

Montana was the 41st state admitted to the United States in 1889. This state lives up to its nickname, "the Treasure State," not only in the varied natural beauty of its mountain ranges and vast plains, but in its mineral wealth as well. Copper, coal, and oil reserves are among the largest in the nation. Large numbers of big game – deer, antelope, bear, moose, mountain goats, and elk – roam freely in the numerous state parks. Three of five entrances to Yellowstone are found in this state. Glacier National Park has more than 50 glaciers lying in steep mountain slopes. The highest waterfall, which drops 400 feet in 8 miles, is on the Missouri River at Great Falls. In 1862 gold was discovered, and the rush was on as lawless mining camps boomed into existence. Indian leaders Crazy Horse, Gall, and Two Moons led Cheyenne and Sioux warriors into history at the Little Bighorn River in 1876. Known as "Custer's Last Stand," 650 men in Custer's regiment and Custer himself were killed by Indian

MONTANA

This quilt block, named "Montana Maze," incorporates a Nine-Patch design in the center.

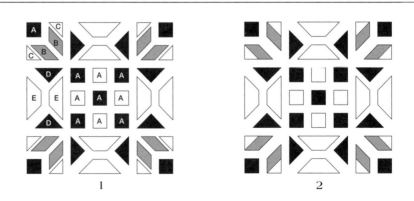

1   2

ASSEMBLY

Begin by laying out all the pieces in this arrangement (1). Sew B and C pieces together (2). Then join square A to these pieced BC sections. Sew A squares together to make the 3 center strips, and sew D triangles to E pieces as shown in (3). Next join these resulting pieced sections into blocks as shown in (4). Then sew these blocks into 3 strips (5). Join these strips to complete this block (6).

QUILT TOP

Arrange these blocks side by side and top to bottom to achieve this pattern. As you can see, the center Nine-Patch stands out and the corners seem to make another very distinct design.

3

4

5

6

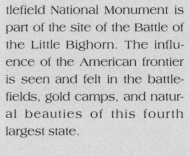

warriors. Today, Custer Battlefield National Monument is part of the site of the Battle of the Little Bighorn. The influence of the American frontier is seen and felt in the battlefields, gold camps, and natural beauties of this fourth largest state.

■ The bitterroot, used by Indians as food, is the state's flower. The starchy root is very long-lived, and even if out of the soil for several years they will begin to grow again when replanted. Short, thick, fleshy pencil-shaped leaves grow on low-growing stalks. The blooms are shades of bright rosy red and have many petals. It grows wild in dry soil or gravel, making them a natural choice for sunny rock gardens. This unusual plant has given its name to a river, valley, and mountain range found in this state.

■ Montana's state tree, the Ponderosa pine, has 3- to 7-inch long needles that grow in a cluster of three. It is valued for its lumber, which is widely used for building, fencing, railroad ties, and construction. Oddly enough, the young shoots, when broken, have an odor like an orange!

■ The Western meadowlark is the state bird for Montana.

Montana pattern – page 138

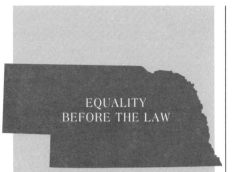

EQUALITY
BEFORE THE LAW

NEBRASKA

This quilt block named "Nebraska" is a complex one. An intriguing collection of triangles, squares, and rectangles form together in this interesting configuration. This block is time-consuming to assemble, but well worth the effort.

NEBRASKA
The Cornhusker State

Nebraska was the 37th state admitted to the United States in 1867. This Midwestern state features Chimney Rock National Historic Site, the Agate Fossil Beds National Monument, and the Scotts Bluff National Monument. Boys Town, a home for neglected and homeless boys founded by Catholic Priest Edward J. Flanagan, is located near Omaha. Two famous Nebraska natives are Gerald Ford and Johnny Carson. Buffalo Bill (William) Cody built a beautiful Victorian home on Scouts Rest Ranch near North Platte. In 1883 he organized the famous Wild West Show bearing his name. Nebraska is nicknamed "the Cornhusker State" from their leading agricultural crop, and because of the cornhusking contest held each fall in farming communities. Although it was considered part of the Great American Desert, irrigation practices have made this state a leader in farming income.

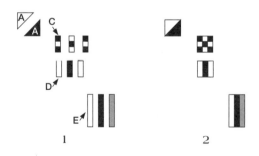

ASSEMBLY

Begin by laying out all the pieces in this arrangement (1). To begin the assembly of the 169 pieces for this block sew dark pattern A triangles and light pattern A triangles together (and the dark and medium triangles). Then sew dark and light pattern C squares together as shown. Sew dark and light D rectangles together. Sew dark, medium, and light E rectangles together. Press all seams toward the dark side (2). Sew strips of pattern pieces C together to form a mini Nine-Patch (3). Lay out all the pieces you have just sewn along with pattern pieces B and F as shown and assemble in strips (4). When you have each strip assembled as shown, sew the strips together. This will make your finished block when the strips have been joined together (5).

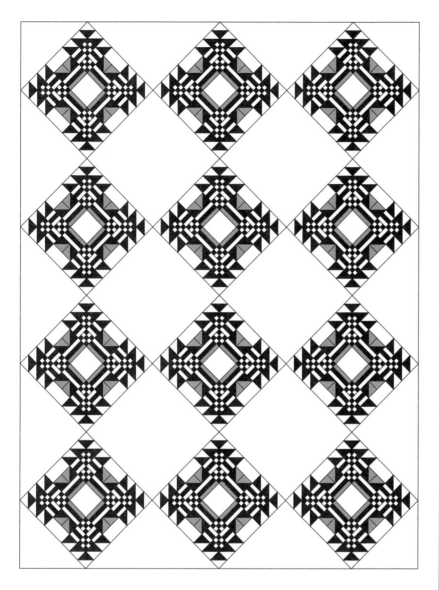

QUILT TOP

Because this quilt block is so involved, it works well when a solid 12" block is placed between each one and turned on point.

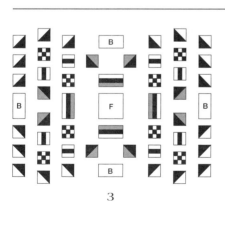

3

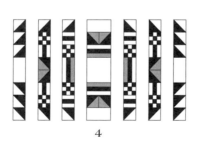

4

5

Nebraska pattern – page 139

■ Goldenrod, a hardy perennial plant, is this state's flower along with Kentucky. It has an erect stalk with yellow sprays of hundreds of tiny, tightly packed yellow flowers at its top. Some species bloom in June, others throughout the summer and late fall. While it is considered a wild weed here in the United States, in Europe it is often planted as a garden flower.

■ Wyoming and Kansas claim the cottonwood as their state tree along with Nebraska. It is in the willow family and grows naturally in and around watercourses. They are excellent shade-making plants, with pale bark that becomes deeply furrowed with age.

■ With so much grain in the Nebraska fields, a natural choice for the state bird is the Western meadowlark. Their food is found in the ample meadows and grainfields of the state. It is also the state bird for Kansas, Montana, North Dakota, Oregon, and Wyoming.

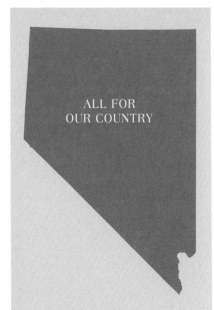

ALL FOR
OUR COUNTRY

NEVADA
The Silver State

Nevada was the 36th state admitted to the United States in 1864. Hoover Dam is a man-made wonder located on the Colorado River near the Arizona-Nevada border. Its reservoir, Lake Mead, is one of the largest man-made lakes. Samuel Clemens spent time here and wrote *Roughing It*, an amusing look at life in Nevada in the 1860's. The transcontinental railroad, which was built primarily by Chinese contract workers, crossed the state. Frontiersman Kit Carson had many adventures here and the capital, Carson City, is named in his honor. The Anasazi, Washo, Paiute, Goshute, and Shoshone Indians lived here and remain an important part of Nevada life. The cowboy culture is still celebrated today at the National Finals Rodeo in Las Vegas. While searching for gold, miners hit the largest silver strike in the world in 1859 near Virginia

NEVADA

The name for this quilt block pattern is "Nevada." Here is an opportunity to make a block with a real three-dimensional design.

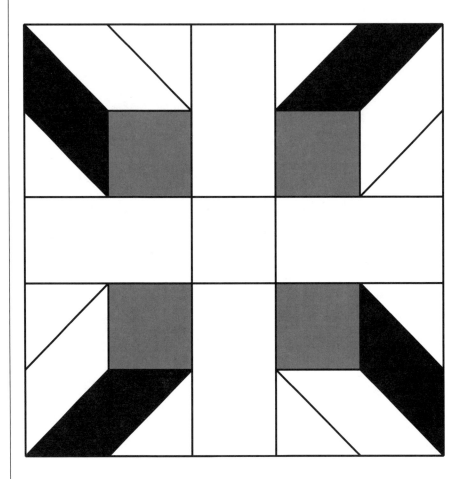

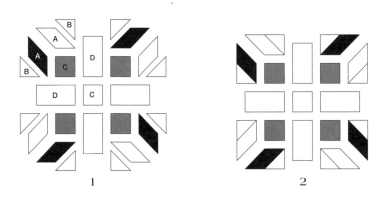

ASSEMBLY

Begin by laying out all the pieces in this arrangement (1). Sew B triangles to A pieces as shown in (2). Join these resulting sections to C squares (3), and then join these sections together to form the 4 pieced corner squares (4). Sew the resulting squares and D rectangles together and then C and D pieces to form 3 strips (5). To finish this block join these strips together (6).

QUILT TOP

Placing this block side by side and top to bottom will give you this secondary design that looks very three dimensional.

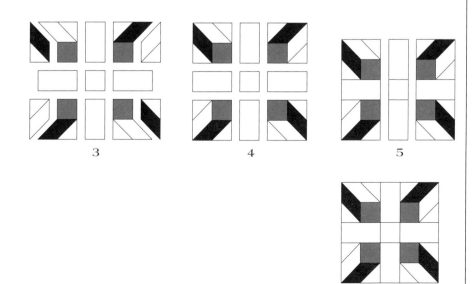

3

4

5

6

City. Named the Comstock Load, prospectors flocked to the area seeking their fortunes. Nevada today produces much of the nation's copper and gold. Another way to strike it rich is in the world-famous casino resorts. Recognized as the gaming capital of the world, it is home to 12 of the 13 largest hotels in the world. Majestic mountains, wide open spaces, and the glitter of casinos highlight the tourist draw to this Rocky Mountain state.

- Sagebrush is Nevada's state flower. It is the most common plant in the desert as it thrives in dry regions. It is a shrubby plant exhibiting leaves covered with silvery down. Its upper leaves are much narrower than the lower ones. Tiny yellow blooms sit tightly against the stems.

- The state tree is the single-leaf piñon. This evergreen produces the same delicious nut as a regular piñon pine. As its name suggests, the needles are set singly along the stem instead of in clusters of two or three.

- The mountain bluebird, unlike its eastern cousin, has a solid blue back and pale blue breast fading to a white belly.

Nevada pattern – page 140

NEW HAMPSHIRE

The name for this quilt block pattern is "New Hampshire's Granite Rock." Like granite, it is a very strong, solid pattern.

LIVE
FREE
OR DIE

NEW HAMPSHIRE
The Granite
State

New Hampshire was the 9th state admitted to the United States in 1788. Among this state's early best-known products were the sturdy Concord Coaches. These vehicles not only helped to open the west, but also improved transportation in Mexico, Canada, South Africa, and Australia. Large deposits of red and gray granite give the state its nickname. Because there are over 50 covered bridges in this tiny state they seem almost a signature for it. Over half of New Hampshire's seacoast is public land. The Strawbery Banke historic district in Portsmouth is one of the most extensive colonial restorations in America. Canterbury Shaker Village, Robert Frost Farm in Derry, and the replica of a French and Indian War bastion, Fort No. 4 in Charleston, all allow tourists to view different life styles and time periods. Saint-Gaudens National Historic Site consists of the home,

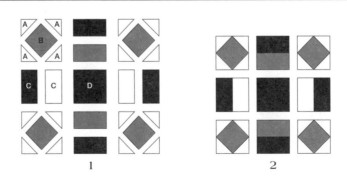

1   2

ASSEMBLY

Begin by laying out all the pieces in this arrangement (1). Sew A triangles to B squares and then attach C rectangles together as shown in (2). Join these resulting squares into 3 strips (3). Finish the block by sewing these strips together (4).

QUILT TOP

When this block is placed side by side and top to bottom it makes a very bold striped design.

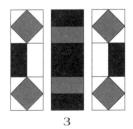

3

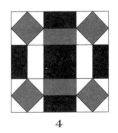

4

gardens, and studio of Augustus Saint-Gaudens, one of the greatest American sculptors. Summer, winter, fall, or spring, this state offers year-round outdoor activities such as picnicking, hunting, fishing, snowmobiling, hiking, and both water and snow skiing. The unspoiled wilderness areas of the White Mountains and over 1,300 lakes provide wondrous scenery as the backdrop for tourist activities.

■ The purple lilac has pyramid-shaped clusters of flowers at the end of small branches. The flower blossoms are very fragrant and the panicles vary in size. Until the early settlers brought them, lilacs were not found here.

■ The state tree is the white birch. Also called canoe birch, it was used by Native Americans to make birch-bark canoes. Common and well-known throughout the North, this tree grows in the open woods and riverbanks. The twigs are thin and droop slightly, and the smooth, chalk-white bark is spotted with horizontal openings.

■ The purple finch, not quite living up to its name, is a reddish-plum color. They often build a frail nest in cedar trees and prefer pine woods and open canyons.

New Hampshire pattern – page 141

LIBERTY
AND
PROSPERITY

NEW JERSEY
The Garden
State

New Jersey was the 3rd state admitted to the United States in 1787. The Delaware River ports on the western edge of this state are host to numerous ocean-going vessels and inland boats. In spite of its nickname, the "Garden State," it leads the nation in chemical production. Many firsts took place here. The first locomotive steam engine in the U.S. was built here, and the first game of organized baseball took place in Hoboken. Thomas Edison invented his electric light bulb and the phonograph in his laboratory at Menlo Park. Samuel Morse developed the electric telegraph near Morristown, and John Holland sailed the first submarine in waters off the shores of this state. The first dinosaur remains unearthed in North America were found in Haddonfield. This small

NEW JERSEY

The name for this quilt block pattern is "New Jersey." It is not difficult to construct and makes a remarkable quilt top.

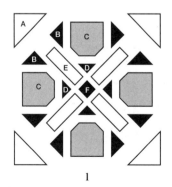

1

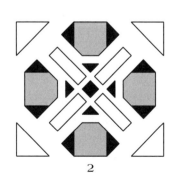

2

ASSEMBLY PAGE

Begin by laying out all the pieces in this arrangement (1). Sew B triangles to C pieces as shown (2). Then connect D triangles to this pieced BC section (3). Make a strip with 2 E rectangles and the F square and sew the remaining E rectangles to pieced BCD sections (4). Sew each pieced BCDE section to a BCD section as shown (5). Then sew these two pieced sections to the EFE section (6). To finish the block sew the corner A triangles to the center pieced section (7).

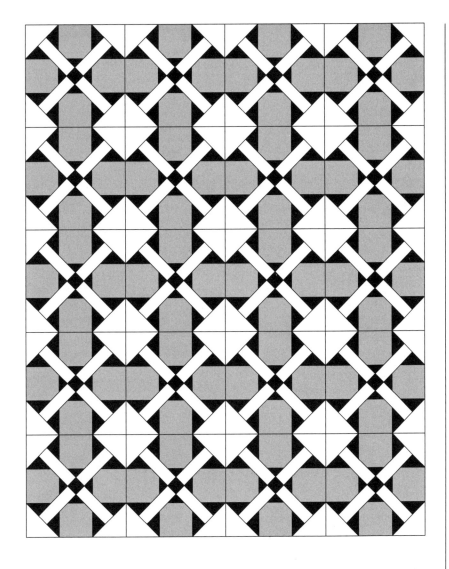

QUILT TOP

When this block is placed side by side and top to bottom it gives a wonderful three-dimensional effect. The light squares formed by the corners of the block (A pieces) and the light rectangles (E pieces) seem to float above the rest of the design.

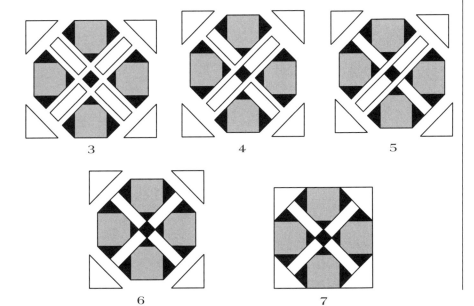

state has many contrasts from sunny beaches on the Atlantic Coast to the winter wonderland of the scenic Kittatinny Mountains to the north. The Delaware Water Gap in the Kittatinny mountain range is a deep narrow gorge that attracts many tourists, and Atlantic City is only one of the resort areas on the great coastal playgrounds.

■ The purple violet is New Jersey's flower. Also known as the sweet violet, it has heart-shaped leaves of mid- to dark-green color. The tiny flowers are shades of purple, and bloom from February to April and sometimes in the autumn. It is an excellent ground cover and grows well in the shade.

■ The state tree is the red oak. It is a common tree of open woods and one of the largest oaks. It is valued not only for its scenic beauty and shade, but for its timber as well.

■ New Jersey and Iowa have the eastern goldfinch as their state bird.

New Jersey pattern – page 142

NEW MEXICO
The Land of Enchantment

New Mexico was the 47th state admitted to the United States in 1912. The capital, Santa Fe, was also the capital of a Spanish province in 1610, making this the oldest seat of government. Mexican trappers and traders came to New Mexico in the early 1800's and Mexico took over the government in 1821. In 1848 the U.S. took control, and Kit Carson led troops to force the Mescalero Apache and Navajo Indians onto reservations. During the late 1800's cattlemen fought for control of Lincoln County. The violence resulted in the death of John G. Tunstall. Billy the Kid and other notorious outlaws took a leading part in what was to become known as the Lincoln County War. This state was brought into the nuclear age when the first atomic bomb was exploded at Trinity Site in 1945. The bombs dropped on Japan later that year were secretly produced in Los Alamos. As you might expect with a state so rich in history,

NEW MEXICO

The name for this quilt block pattern is "New Mexico." With its center checkerboards and corner triangle designs, it may look difficult but is actually quite easy to assemble.

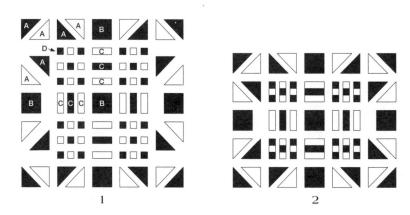

1   2

ASSEMBLY

Begin by laying out all the pieces in this arrangement (1). Sew D squares into strips as shown (2). Sew C rectangles together to make squares. Connect A triangles together to make squares (3). Then sew these squares into strips (4). To finish the block sew these strips together (5).

QUILT TOP

Setting this block side by side and top to bottom will give you this quilt top. It is a very dramatic design, and when joined together the small corner triangles form a square on point.

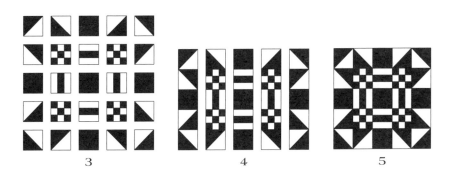

3   4   5

many Spanish fiestas, Native American ceremonies, and rodeos are held every year. Carlsbad Caverns is one of the world's great natural wonders, and the Puyé cliff dwellings are an ancient manmade attraction. Natural beauty abounds in this scenic state from the large desert basin of the Jornada del Muerto to the snow-capped peaks of the Rocky Mountains.

■ The yucca, an evergreen with lengthy strap-shaped leaves, is long lived and thrives well in poor sandy soil. They flower best during hot summers. The creamy white blossoms grow at the top of a tall woody trunk. It is generally pest free and requires no pruning, making it a very popular ornamental.

■ The state tree is the piñon pine. It produces a pine nut that is considered a delicacy. It is a low-growing, drought-resistant tree found on mesas and mountainsides.

■ The roadrunner has a peculiar toe arrangement on its foot with two toes in front and two toes behind, making it hard to track his direction. In horse-and-buggy days the bird delighted in running along the road ahead of vehicles. When it wants to stop it will erect and spread its tail. This pattern of racing swiftly and stopping suddenly made it a natural choice for a cartoon character.

New Mexico pattern – page 143

NEW YORK

The name for this quilt block pattern is "New York Flag." It is the most patriotic design of all 50 states.

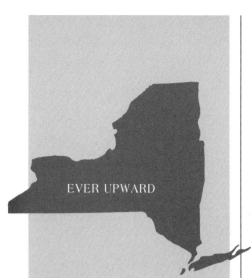

NEW YORK
The Empire State

New York was the 11th state admitted to the United States in 1788. It is only natural to think of New York City when talking about this state. This city is the largest in the nation and the fourth largest in the world. It is a wonderful cultural center driven by genius and creativity with many theaters and museums. It has been host to two World's Fairs and many cultural festivals, historical celebrations, and sports competitions. It is one of the world's busiest seaports, with the Statue of Liberty standing in its harbor, and is the headquarters for the United Nations. "Gold Coast" estates like the John S. Phipps mansion, featuring formal gardens, statuary, and Georgian architecture, rival manors in Europe. The state is also rich in natural beauty. It is filled with meandering rivers, clear blue lakes, rugged mountains, and picturesque farmland. Travelers from around

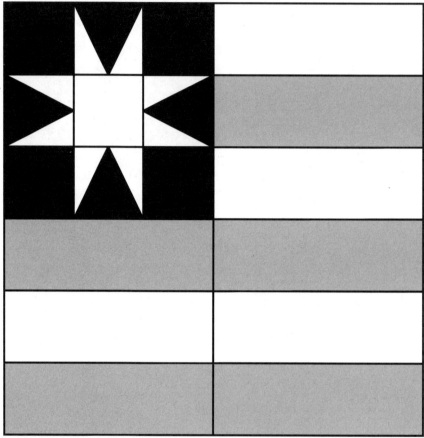

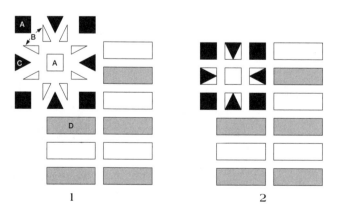

1   2

ASSEMBLY
Begin by laying out all the pieces in this arrangement (1). Sew B pieces to C triangles (2). Then attach A squares to these pieced sections as in (3). Sew these pieced rectangles and D pieces into two strips (4). To finish the block sew these two strips together (5).

QUILT TOP

This is one of the easiest quilt blocks to assemble and it really gives a very primitive country feeling. Setting a 12" block between each flag block allows you to bring in additional colors if you like.

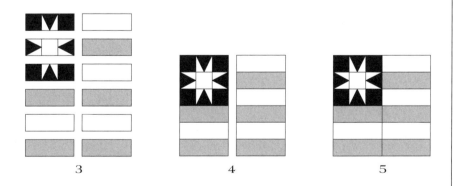

3　　　　　　　4　　　　　　　5

the world are spellbound at the sight and sound of the rushing waters of Niagara Falls. From the high peaks of the Adirondacks to the pine barrens of Long Island, opportunities for summer and winter sports and tourism abound.

■ The rose is New York's state flower, and what a wonderful choice it is! There is a never-ending list of species of roses, but generally all are hardy and deciduous. The hybrid tea rose freely produces flowers and has a long flowering season from June to October, which makes it a favorite. The blooms are generally double and bowl-shaped and open from a shapely conical bud. Some are fragrant and all have a prickly stem.

■ The state tree is the sugar maple.

■ The vivid color of the bluebird, New York's state bird, is due to refraction rather than pigment in his feathers, and he looks bluest in bright sunlight. He has a rosy chestnut breast shading to white underparts. He belongs to the thrush family and has a cheerful soft warble.

New York pattern – page 144

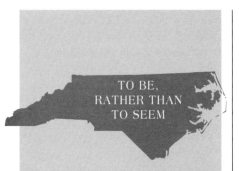

TO BE,
RATHER THAN
TO SEEM

NORTH CAROLINA
The Tar Heel State

North Carolina was the 12th state admitted to the United States in 1789. During the Civil War retreating Confederate troops left North Carolina troops to fend for themselves. The North Carolinians decided they should have put tar on the retreating soldiers heels to keep them in place. Since then the nickname "tar heels" has "stuck" with the state. It is the leading tobacco-producing state, and also produces more cloth and wooden furniture than any other state. The Smokey and Blue Ridge Mountains border the western portion and turn into the rolling hills of the Piedmont Plateau as you move eastward. Biltmore Estate near Asheville covers about 12,000 acres. The chief feature of this compound is the Biltmore House, an early French Renaissance masterpiece. Old Salem was founded by the Moravians in 1766 and is today a treasury of fine old restored buildings opened as exhibits. Bakers, cobblers, weavers, and others go about their business as if it were still 1766. Many lovely waterfalls fed by mountain streams and rivers add to the beauty of southwestern North

NORTH CAROLINA

The name for this quilt block pattern is "North Carolina Star." Piecing this block may seem awkward at first, but it is not too difficult after the first block is finished.

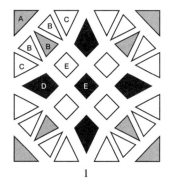

1   2

ASSEMBLY

Begin by laying out all the pieces in this arrangement (1). Sew B pieces together as shown in (2). Then attach C triangles to these pieced sections. Sew D pieces to E blocks. Then sew remaining E blocks together to form the center strip (3). Attach A triangles to CB pieced sections to make corner sections and sew pieced sections DE to E center strip to form center star (4). To finish the block sew the corner sections to the center star (5).

QUILT TOP

Arrange these blocks side by side horizontally and top to bottom vertically to make this quilt top. It almost gives a circular feeling to the design.

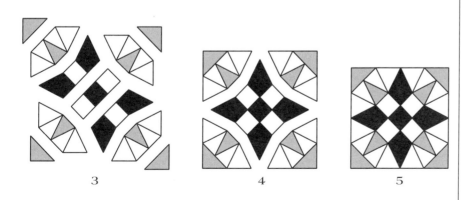

3   4   5

Carolina. The first airplane flight took place on the sand dunes at Kitty Hawk. The Outer Banks with its reefs and sand bars have sent many ships to the bottom of the ocean giving Cape Hatteras the nickname of "the Grave-yard of the Atlantic." Dunes, forest, marshlands, and miles of unspoiled beaches make up the 736 acre Hammocks Beach State Park on the south-ern coast. The "lost colony," an early English colony, land-ed on Roanoke Island in 1587. Three years later a supply expedition found they had dis-appeared with the only clue, the word Croatoan, carved in a tree. Virginia Dare, the first child born to English parents in America, vanished along with the others. It remains today the nation's oldest unsolved mystery.

■ The flowering dogwood is the state's choice for its flower. It is also the state flower or tree for Virginia and Missouri.

■ The state tree is the pine. It is an evergreen with long thin needles and no real bloom. Its seeds are developed within a cone. These trees are tolerant of poor soil and produce tur-pentine and resins.

■ The cardinal is North Caroli-na's state bird. These birds are non-migratory and found year round in woodlands and swamps as well as suburbs.

North Carolina pattern – page 145

NORTH DAKOTA

The name for this quilt block pattern is "North Dakota." The central star may be emphasized by the use of your materials.

NORTH DAKOTA
The Flickertail State

North Dakota was the 39th state admitted to the United States in 1889. Nearly all of this state is covered with ranches and farms that produce large quantities of flaxseed, barley, and rye, and only Kansas raises more wheat. Oil was discovered in 1951 and quickly became the most valuable mineral here. As well as oil, large coal reserves, and sand, gravel, and clay deposits fuel the state's economy. The annual Sodbusters Days at Fort Ransom State Park brings the era of horse-powered farming to life. The Red River Valley is the most populous region of the state. It is an ethnic melting-pot with festivals held throughout the year. In the lakes and garden region the capital, Minot, is host to the internationally known Norsk Hostfest.This Scandinavian festival that takes place in October ranks among the top 100 events in North America. At Fort Totten, cowboys and Indians, two cultures that met more than a century ago on the plains of the Dakota Territory, come alive. The rodeo and pow wow activities of the

1   2

ASSEMBLY
Begin by laying out all the pieces in this arrangement (1). Sew A and B pieces together and then C and A pieces together. Also sew remaining A pieces to D pieces (2). Next sew these pieced sections together as shown in (3). Sew the center star AD together (4), and complete the block by sewing the corner sections ABC to the center star (5).

QUILT TOP

Placing a 12" medium color block between these quilt blocks and turning them on point will result in a quilt top like this.

3

4

5

festival take place not more than a hundred yards apart. Lt. Col. George Armstrong Custer was posted to Fort Lincoln in 1873 and the Custer House, his private quarters left virtually intact, today has daily tours during the summer months. The Peace Garden is a 2,300 acre botanical wonder near Kunseith in the Turtle Mountains. Today North Dakota has more wildlife refuges than any other state. Each fall one of the most spectacular events in nature takes place here when tens of thousands of ducks and geese gather for their trip south. Buffalo, once hunted almost to extinction, are now found in protected herds. Deer, elk, moose, antelope, coyotes, and even prairie dogs contribute to the North Dakota Watchable Wildlife Program.

- The wild prairie rose, with stems that climb over walls and fences, is the state flower. It blooms in early summer with roses that are first a deep pink and change to white when in full bloom.

- The state tree is the American elm. Well known because it is found in woods, fields, and town streets, now it is menaced by insects and Dutch elm disease. It is easy to identify at a distance by its vase shape form.

- The Western meadowlark is the state bird.

North Dakota pattern – page 146

WITH GOD,
ALL THINGS
ARE POSSIBLE

OHIO
The Buckeye
State

Ohio was the 17th state admitted to the United States in 1803. In the early 1800's winemaking vineyards were planted, and today this state grows more varieties of grapes than California. There are more than 46 wineries across the state producing many wine varieties. Apples have made Ohio an important fruit-producing state since the days of Johnny Appleseed. Because Ohio has large deposits of coal, salt, and other minerals, an abundant supply of water, and is centrally located, it has been very attractive to large industries. Holmes, Wayne, and Tuscarawas counties are home to the largest population of Amish in the world. Astronauts John Glenn and Neil Armstrong were from this state, and John Glenn is currently representing his state in the U.S. Senate. The Appalachian foothills in the southeast have some of the state's most beautiful terrain and natural splendor. Lake Erie to the

OHIO

The name for this quilt block pattern is "Ohio Trail." Since the Ohio Star pattern is so common, I decided to use a different pattern. It is very easy to make with only two pattern pieces and straight line assembly.

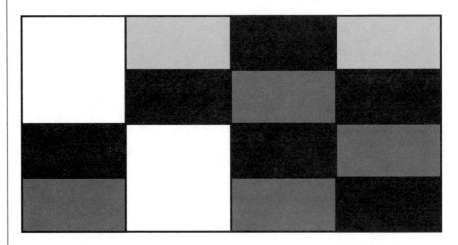

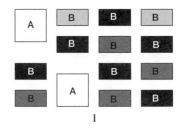

1

ASSEMBLY

Begin by laying out all the pieces in this arrangement (1). Sew these rectangles and squares into strips as in (2). Next sew these strips together to finish this block (3).

QUILT TOP

Placing these quilt blocks side by side and staggering each successive row by half a block will result in this quilt top. You can plainly see the trail running at an angle down the design.

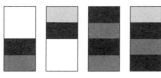

2

3

north and the Ohio River to the south provide opportunities for many water sports. Ohio is practically a mecca for antiques and collectibles fans. Museums specializing in dolls, toys, Heisey glass, ceramics, paperweights and glass, railroad, cola, tools, football, and classic cars as well as art, science, and industry are found throughout this state.

- As beautiful as it is fragrant, the scarlet carnation is Ohio's state flower. It was President William McKinley's favorite flower and Ohio, named it in his honor. President McKinley was born in Niles, Ohio in 1843. Six other presidents were born in this state in addition to McKinley. They were Ulysses S. Grant, Rutherford B. Hayes, James A. Garfield, Benjamin Harrison, William Howard Taft, and Warren G. Harding.

- The state tree is the buckeye, giving the state its nickname. Because these trees were plentiful the early pioneers used them to build log cabins. These trees are unusual in that their fruit is inedible and their compound leaves grow from a thick twig with leaflets radiating out from a center point like the fingers of your hand.

- The cardinal is the state bird.

Ohio pattern – page 147

OKLAHOMA
The Sooner State

Oklahoma was the 46th state admitted to the United States in 1907. It is a leading state in oil production. In 1889 the first productive oil well was drilled, and today oil derricks dot almost all of the state with pipelines carrying crude oil to refineries. In 70 of Oklahoma's 77 counties deposits of oil or natural gas are found. From the picturesque musical *Oklahoma* to the description of drought conditions in the *Grapes of Wrath*, from the National Cowboy Hall of Fame and Western Heritage Center to the Federal Aeronautics Authority Aeronautical Center in Oklahoma City, this state has its share of contrasts. The Chisholm Trail runs across the state and was used by cattle drivers to move herds to Kansas in the late 1800's. Paintings by Frederic Remington and Charles Russell hang in the Woolaroc Museum close to Bartlesville along with many displays of southwest history. The Will Rogers Memorial Building is a stone ranch house in Claremore featuring exhibits about Native Americans and pio-

OKLAHOMA

The name for this quilt block pattern is "Oklahoma Twister." It is fairly easy to assemble with only three pattern pieces.

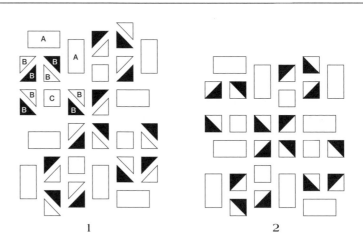

1   2

ASSEMBLY
Begin by laying out all the pieces in this arrangement (1). Sew B triangles together as shown in (2). Next make pieced blocks of pieced squares BB, C squares, and A rectangles as in (3). Sew these pieced blocks and remaining C squares and A rectangles into strips (4). To complete the block sew these strips together (5).

QUILT TOP

Placing these quilt blocks side by side and top to bottom will display this traditional overall design for a quilt top.

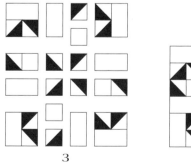

3

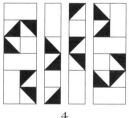

4

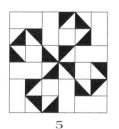

5

neers as well as Rogers himself. The Tsa-La-Gi Indian Village re-creates an ancient Cherokee village, a reminder of the large Indian heritage of this state. In the 1820's a large portion of Oklahoma was given to the Cherokee, Choctaw, Creek, Chickasaw, and Seminole tribes as they reached the end of the arduous and infamous Trail of Tears. As tribes were given individual allotments of their lands, Oklahoma was opened to settlers and the land rush was on.

- The state flower is mistletoe. It is a parasite plant that finds a host tree and grows into a thickly branched clump with thick yellow-green leaves and creamy white berries. It is an evergreen with tiny yellow flowers blooming in February and March. The use of this plant throughout history as charms and in ceremonies is probably the basis for the tradition of forfeiting a kiss if you are found standing under it at Christmastime.

- The state tree is the redbud. Hardy and colorful, this favorite ornamental blooms early in the spring. In spite of its name the blossoms are a beautiful lavender to purple and almost cover the tree. Tolerant of shade, it has thin heart-shaped leaves that turn bright yellow in the fall.

- The scissor-tail flycatcher is the state bird, and is responsible for getting rid of many harmful insects. This elegant as well as useful bird has a pronounced forked tail that may grow from 10 to 14 inches in length.

Oklahoma pattern – page 148

OREGON
The Beaver State

Oregon was the 33rd state admitted to the United States in 1859. Oregon is a state that supplies a large amount of the nation's lumber. The most important manufacturing industry is wood processing. Its vast wonderful forests also draw over 10 million tourists a year. The Willamette Valley, a welcome end for frontiersmen that traveled on the Oregon Trail in the last century, is today a busy industrial, agricultural, and trade area of the state. Sea Lions Cave on the Pacific Coast, Columbia River Gorge through the Cascade Mountains, Crater Lake National Park, and the Bonneville Dam with its series of fish ladders are only a few of this state's tourist attractions. World-famous orchards abound inland and in the north-central section of the state wheat comprises a valuable agricultural treasure. The climate is the contributing factor for the state's beautiful azaleas, laurels, rhododendron, daffodils, gladiolus, iris, lilies and tulips. Sandy beaches, rugged cliffs, and protected harbors make

OREGON

This block, named "Oregon," is an interesting and unique little pattern. Because of the diagonal pieces within this design, a striped or directional material for these pieces would be a good choice to give it a very different look.

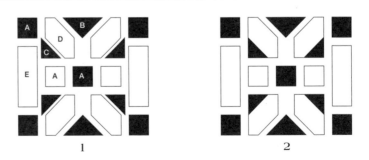

ASSEMBLY

Begin by laying out all the pieces in this arrangement (1). Sew pattern pieces C to pattern pieces D as shown (2), then sew these two sections together and add triangle B. Sew center blocks A together (3). Sew sections BCD to each side of a strip A section and sew A squares to E rectangles to form 3 strips (4). Then sew these 3 assembled strips together to form the completed block (5).

QUILT TOP

Place this block side by side but rotate every other block 90°. On the next row move this block arrangement over by a single block and this quilt top will come together.

3   4   5

up the western Pacific coast of the state. The federal government has set aside 10 areas in Oregon's national forests to be preserved as natural wilderness areas. This state has so many natural rarities that it is also known as the Pacific Wonderland.

- The state flower is the Oregon grape or holly grape. This hardy little shrub is in the barberry family and grows in abundance in the Northwest. This is an evergreen plant that closely resembles a holly, but in the fall the leaves change from a dark green to a rich bronze. In the spring small bunches of bright yellow blooms grow to develop into grape-like bunches of blue-violet fruit.

- It seems only natural that the Douglas fir is the state tree since Oregon's economy is so closely related to timber. This tree provides the majority of the lumber harvested from this state and is the source of more lumber than any other tree in North America. It is not a true fir tree but rather a cone-bearing, soft-wood pine tree that can grow to be more than 200 feet tall and 3 to 4 feet in diameter. As you may expect, conservation practices are very popular in this state.

- As with Nebraska, Montana, North Dakota, and Kansas, the Western meadowlark is this Pacific state's bird.

Oregon pattern – page 149

The name for this quilt block pattern is "Pennsylvania Pineapple." With only light and dark tones to consider this is a very bold design.

PENNSYLVANIA
The Keystone State

Pennsylvania was the 2nd state admitted to the United States in 1787. The Declaration of Independence, which granted freedom from England to the original 13 colonies, was signed at Independence Hall in Philadelphia in 1776. Years later, in 1787, the Constitution of the United States was adopted and signed in this historic city. During the Revolutionary War, George Washington and his troops suffered through a bitter winter at Valley Forge. Gettysburg, nestled in Adams County, is filled with over 20 museums and attractions, as well as colorful fruit orchards, covered bridges, and mountain scenary. From the steel processing centers at Pittsburgh and Bethlehem to the quaint Amish communities at Bird-In-Hand, this state has much to offer in addition to historical treasures. It ranks third in nation-wide coal production behind Kentucky and West Virginia, and supplies all of the hard (anthracite) coal produced in the U.S. It also leads in the production of pig iron and steel. The nation's first commercially successful oil well was drilled near

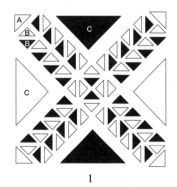

1

2

ASSEMBLY

Begin by laying out all the pieces in this arrangement (1). Sew all A triangles together to make squares as in (2). Attach these squares to make strips (3). Sew these strips together to make larger strips and sew A triangles to the ends of each strip (4). Connect C triangles to each side of the pieced sections to make corner pieced triangles (5). To complete the block sew these resulting triangles to the center strip (6).

QUILT TOP

Placing these quilt blocks side by side and top to bottom results in a very striking and traditional style design. Because there are such large triangle pieces (C), this would be a good choice to use a dramatic fabric if you wanted a different look or to give the impression that the smaller pieced strips are "floating" above this fabric.

3

4

5

6

Titusville by Edwin Drake, and today the northwest area has over 30,000 producing oil wells. The first federal mint was opened in Philadelphia in 1792, and currently conducts tours daily. The Rockville Bridge, which stretches across the Susquehanna River, is one of the world's largest stone arch bridges. The Blue Ridge, Appalachian, and Allegheny Mountains are found across this entire state and provide a wealth of tourist attractions. The Pocono Mountains provide the most spectacular waterfalls in the eastern United States.

- It seems natural, because the majority of this state is mountainous, that the state flower should be the mountain laurel. This woody shrub has glossy dark-green leaves that remain on the plant throughout the year. Blossoms are rose-red flower clusters found at the end of the stems.

- The state tree is the hemlock. A member of the pine family, this tree is easily transplanted and very popular as an ornamental in addition to its use in construction and as pulp wood.

- The ruffed grouse is the choice for the state bird. The name comes from the ruff around his neck that is purplish black. Found in the deep woods, it is a large chicken-like bird that makes a very distinctive sound when taking flight. It is easily recognizable not only by size but also by the tuft on top of its head, and the fan-shaped tail with a broad black band.

Pennsylvania pattern – page 151

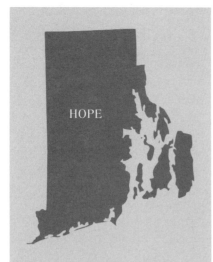

RHODE ISLAND
Little Rhody

Rhode Island was the 13th state admitted to the United States in 1790. Providence is the leading jewelry manufacturing center in the U.S., and production of jewelry and silverware is the state's most important manufacturing activity. A rich nautical heritage is evident in this smallest state. It has a large concentration of the nation's historic landmarks. The "Mile of History" in Providence features scores of 18th century homes along Benefit Street. Newport has been the home of the America's Cup for 50 years, and the South County beaches are host to a panorama of spectacular turn-of-the-century homes. One of the most ornate buildings in the U.S. is found in this state. It is *Marble House* built for William K. Vanderbilt in 1892. Nearby is *The Beaches*, which was built for Cornelius Vanderbilt and is one of the nation's most famous buildings. The annual Spring Bulb Display at Blithewold Gardens and

RHODE ISLAND

The name for this quilt block pattern is "Rhode Island Maple Leaf" and is very appropriate since the state tree is the red maple.

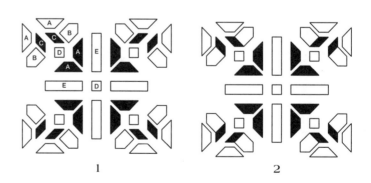

1   2

ASSEMBLY

Begin by laying out all the pieces in this arrangement (1). Sew C to B pieces as shown (2). Then attach light A pieces to pieced CB sections and center dark A pieces together as shown (3). Attach square D to pieced ABC sections (4). Sew ABC sections to ABCD sections (5). To construct corner squares sew pieced dark AA sections to pieced ABCD corners (6). Make strips by sewing these pieced corner squares to rectangle E and remaining E pieces to center D square (7). To complete this block sew these resulting strips together (8).

QUILT TOP

Placing these quilt blocks side by side and top to bottom produces an almost kaleidoscope effect, depending on the material you use in the outside corner pieces (A). It also looks as though the center rectangles form a sashing that criss-crosses the quilt top.

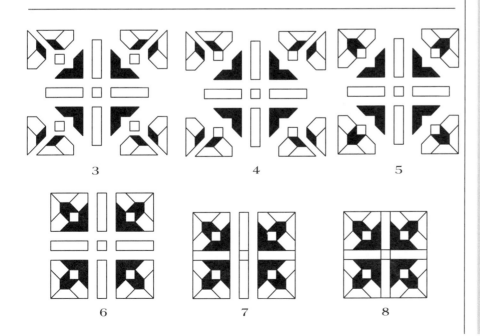

3   4   5

6   7   8

Arboretum showcases over 50,000 flowering spring flowers and draws both horticulturists and tourists. With its rocky Atlantic coast and wealth of Colonial buildings and historic sites, this state has a true appreciation of the impact of tourism.

- The state flower is the violet. The tiny purple flowers of this low-growing plant often bloom twice a year.

- The state tree is the red maple. This tree lives up to its name by not only turning a gorgeous scarlet in the fall, but by displaying blunt red leaf buds in the spring and clusters of red and orange flowers that hang from reddish twigs. The leaves gradually turn from early spring red to full summer green before returning to the familiar fall color. The wood is soft and close grained and used for many woodenware projects.

- The Rhode Island red was the natural choice for the state bird. This fowl was the result of breeding experiments at Little Compton. Extremely hardy, the hen is a good egg producer.

Rhode Island pattern – page 152

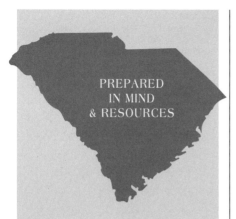

SOUTH CAROLINA
The Palmetto State

South Carolina was the 8th state admitted to the United States in 1788. This "land of opposites" stretches from the Atlantic coast where the pirate Blackbeard preyed in the early 1700's to the lofty Blue Ridge Mountains where the British were defeated at the Battle of Kings Mountain. Charleston and Charleston Harbor is an historic area in this state, and boasts one of the oldest museums, The Charleston Museum, which was founded in 1773. The most famous seaside resort is Myrtle Beach. Some of the nation's most beautiful gardens are found in South Carolina. These include Cyprus Gardens, with lagoons lined with tall, stately Cyprus trees; Middleton Place Gardens, the oldest landscaped garden in the U.S.; and Magnolia Gardens, with over 500 varieties of flowers and trees. The leading agricultural cash crop is still tobacco, with soybeans and cotton as second and third. The textile industry has played a major role in the economy of this state. With

SOUTH CAROLINA

The name for this quilt block pattern is "South Carolina." This block requires close attention to assembly but the results are worth the extra effort.

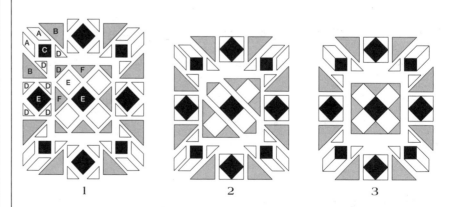

1 2 3

ASSEMBLY

Begin by laying out all the pieces in this arrangement (1). Sew light D triangles to sides of dark E squares and attach A pieces to dark C squares. Attach light E squares to center dark E square and then attach triangle D to the ends of this pieced strip. Also attach triangles D and F to remaining light E squares (2). To complete the center square sew DEF corners to ED strip. Attach A light pieces to AC sections (3). Sew light D triangles to AC pieced sections on one side only

QUILT TOP

A secondary design is achieved by placing these quilt blocks side by side and top to bottom. While this block is time consuming to piece, the resulting quilt top is very striking and a great choice for a scrap quilt.

4

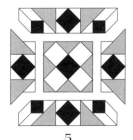

5

6

7

and then attach this section to B triangles (4). Attach remaining light D triangles to pieced sections BED (5). Connect pieced side sections BED to center pieced square DEF (6). To complete this block sew top and bottom sections to the center pieced section (7).

over 435 mills, it is second only to North Carolina in textile production. Cotton, silk and wool as well as orlon, dacron, rayon, glass, and plastic fibers are manufactured here. In the early 1960's, production of man-made fabrics began to increase and today these fabrics are South Carolina's leading textile product.

- The state flower, the yellow jessamine, blooms profusely in early spring. This delicate, yellow funnel-shaped flower grows on a woody vine that is a tenacious climber. Its fragrance is similar to the true jasmine, and its leaves are evergreen with a shiny finish.

- The state tree is the palmetto. Commonly referred to as the cabbage palmetto, it is an attractive feature of the coastal areas of South Carolina, Georgia, Florida, and North Carolina. The large leafbuds are highly prized as a salad vegetable and are used in making pickles and relishes.

- The Carolina wren has a conspicuous white stripe above its eye. They are rusty brown with a buff colored underside. These small birds will sing in all seasons and weather, day or night.

South Carolina pattern – page 153

SOUTH DAKOTA
The Sunshine State

South Dakota was the 40th state admitted to the United States in 1889. Mount Rushmore National Memorial is found in the Black Hills of this state, and the Crazy Horse Memorial near Custer is still under construction. In Mitchell the Corn Palace is covered with murals made of different colored corn and is redecorated each fall. Over 80 percent of the state's income production comes from agriculture. This state today supplies over one fourth of the nation's gold supply. Deadwood was a resulting boomtown of the 1876 gold rush. Boothill Cemetery is found in this infamous town and some of the Western celebrities buried there include Calamity Jane and Wild Bill Hickock. George Custer and Sitting Bull also lived and died in this adventurous state. Several defense projects were built here during the 1960's, and today many missile sights in the western part of the state are directed from Ellsworth Air Force Base. The geographic center of the U. S. is found in

SOUTH DAKOTA

The name for this quilt block pattern is "South Dakota." It features four pinwheel designs, and with only four pattern pieces is easy to put together. A warning, though, you must pay close attention to the color of the A triangles around the D squares to keep the pattern shown here.

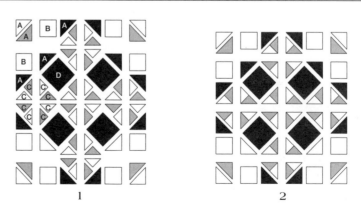

1   2

ASSEMBLY

Begin by laying out all the pieces in this arrangement (1). Sew light C triangles to medium C triangles as shown in (2). Sew A triangles together, pieced C triangles to A triangles, pieced AA squares to B squares, and pieced C triangles and A triangles to D squares (3). Sew these pieced segments into strips (4). Finish the block by sewing these strips together to form the South Dakota design (5).

QUILT TOP

Placing these blocks side by side and top to bottom produces an arrangement that, as with many of these American blocks, fools the eye by forming another design where its corners meet. Note that with this quilt top every other row is reversed to take full advantage of the odd color arrangement at the center of this block. This odd arrangement allows for the alternating rows of circular and cross designs as shown.

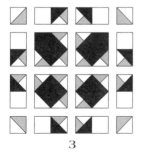

3

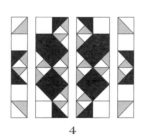

4

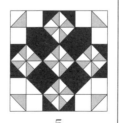

5

this state 17 miles west of Castle Rock. The great lakes of South Dakota are man-made and offer many water sports. White-tailed deer, bighorn sheep, and one of the nation's largest herds of buffalo are added attractions to the natural beauties found in this Midwestern state.

- South Dakota's state flower, the American pasque flower, is thought to have been given its name because it blooms in early spring (close to Pass-over), or because dye made from this plant was used for coloring Easter eggs. This flower has no true petals, but, instead, it has inch-long sepals.

- The Black Hills spruce is the state tree. As with all spruces, their needles, four-sided and nearly square in cross section, are arranged in compact spirals around the twigs. The cones hang down and mature in one season.

- The ring-necked pheasant, the state bird, was imported from China and made themselves at home here around 1880 after several earlier attempts failed to naturalize them. The male has a bare head that is scarlet at the sides. His plumage is a rich mixture of golden browns barred with black. Peacock blue feathers with reflective purple and bronze lights cover his neck with a distinctive collar of white that makes a ring around it. Here in South Dakota these birds are often raised on farms and then released to provide a good hunting season.

South Dakota pattern – page 154

TENNESSEE

The name for this quilt pattern is "Tennessee Circles" and what a great design it is! When taken a step at a time it is not too difficult to assemble, and the finished project is really unique and intriguing.

TENNESSE
The Volunteer State

Tennessee was the 16th state admitted to the United States in 1796. Roughly half this state's land area is used in farming and forestry to produce hardwood lumber, beef cattle, dairy farms, and tobacco. Its most valuable minerals are marble, limestone, and zinc. Coal is Tennessee's second-ranking income-producing mineral. Nashville, the capital, is home to the Grand Ole Opry, the longest continuously running live radio program in the world. It has broadcast every Friday and Saturday night since 1925, contributing to Nashville's nickname, "Music City U.S.A." Memphis is the home of two extraordinary tourists attractions, Mud Island (a 52 acre river park) and the Pyramid (a multi-story sports and special events facility). The Great Smokey Mountains stretch across the eastern portion of the state. Its highest point, Clingman's Dome, is a breathtaking sight in more ways than one. Knoxville is home to the University of Tennessee and was host to the 1982 World's Fair. The Sunsphere, a 266-foot tall tower topped by a golden glass globe, symbolized the theme of energy. In 1812 the worst earthquake in American history took place

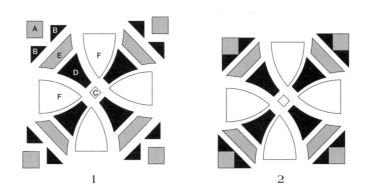

1   2

ASSEMBLY

Begin by laying out all the pieces in this arrangement (1). Sew B triangles to A squares as shown (2). Sew each pieced triangle to each E piece (3) and then sew these pieced segments (ABE) to D pieces (4). Then sew F pieces to each side of 2 opposite segments (ABED) and connect the other 2 opposite segments (ABED) together at the center with square C (5). Finish the block by sewing the corner segments (ABEDF) to the center segment (ABEDC) (6).

QUILT TOP

Placing this quilt block side by side and top to bottom produces this arrangement. It makes a definite circular design, and a seemingly underlaying lattice with squares in the center of the lattice-crossed pieces.

3

4

5

6

in northwestern Tennessee. It caused the Mississippi River to run backwards and in the resulting depression Reelfoot Lake was formed. Reelfoot Lake State Fish and Game Preserve was established in 1925 and now boasts the largest bald eagle population in the U.S.

■ Very hardy and beautiful, the iris is the state's flower. The bloom has three distinct petals which stand up and three sepals that bend down with a golden "beard" laying on each.

■ The tulip poplar was chosen for the state tree because it was used by pioneers to build their houses and barns as they moved and settled into Tennessee. The tree may reach a height of 200 feet with as much as 50 to 100 feet of trunk without a branch, making it an excellent choice as building material. The flowers are green-orange in color and tulip-shaped, and the leaf is very distinctive with a broad notch at the tip.

■ As with Texas, Mississippi, and Arkansas, the state bird is the mockingbird. This North American species has a melodious song of its own, but gets its name from its ability to skillfully mimic the songs of other birds.

Tennessee pattern – page 155

FRIENDSHIP

TEXAS
The Lone Star
State

Texas was the 28th state admitted to the United States in 1845. Though Texans may argue the point, they are the second largest state in the Union. Texas is more than 220 times larger than Rhode Island, the smallest state. Over the years, Spain, Mexico, France, the Republic of Texas, the Confederate States of America, and finally the United States have been the governing bodies of this oil-rich state. Headquarters for all manned spacecraft projects of NASA are based at the Lyndon B. Johnson Space Center near Houston, the largest city in this state. The most recognizable monument in Texas has to be the Alamo in San Antonio, and one of the most infamous events in U.S. history was the assassination of President Kennedy in Dallas on November 22, 1963. The Texas State Fair, the largest annual fair in the U.S., is held in October in Dallas. Texas is a leading state in

TEXAS

The name for this quilt pattern is "Texas Treasure." Though it looks somewhat complicated, it is actually simple and easy to assemble and features a unique design with a large center block.

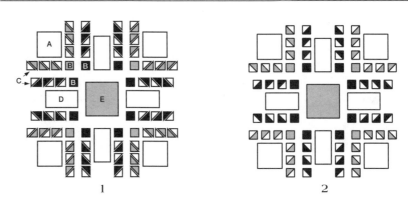

1   2

ASSEMBLY

Begin by laying out all the pieces in this arrangement (1). Sew triangles C together as shown (2). Sew these pieced blocks together to make strips (3) and then sew strips to squares A (4). Sew pieced strips to D rectangles and CB strips to CA pieces (5). Connect these pieced squares into strips with E at the center (6). Sew these strips together to complete the blocks (7).

QUILT TOP

Turn this quilt block on point and place a medium colored 12" block in between each to achieve this design. This arrangement would be a good choice for featuring that wonderful piece of yard goods you have been saving.

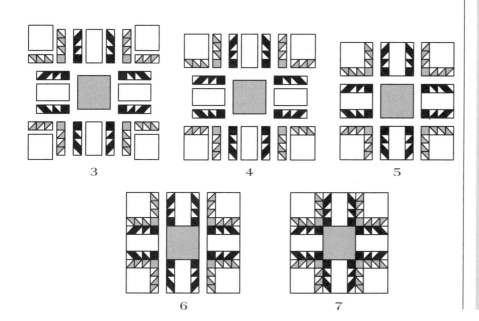

mineral production, ranking first in oil production. In the agricultural field, beef cattle are the largest source of income. This incredibly vast state features the Padre Island National Seashore, Big Bend National Park within the great bend of the Rio Grande River, Guadalupe Mountains National Park, Sabine National Forest, and over 80 more state parks. With a wild and western influence and breathtaking natural beauty, Texas has much to offer tourists no matter the season.

- The bluebonnet, a wild lupine, grows only in Texas, making it a natural choice for this state's flower. Bright blue-violet blooms grow in a long cluster on a stem about a foot tall. Lupine leaves and stems are covered with silky hairs, and the leaves "sleep" at night by drooping around the stem or pointing upward, depending on the species.

- The pecan tree, a native southern hickory, is the state tree. It is an important cultivated crop tree that is also planted as an ornamental. It grows to be from 80 to 100 feet tall and the long nut it produces grows within a thin slightly winged husk.

- The state bird is the mockingbird. This western species is slightly larger and has a little more white on its wings than the eastern bird.

Texas pattern – page 157

INDUSTRY

UTAH
The Beehive
State

Utah was the 45th state admitted to the United States in 1896. From the Balanced Rock in Arches National Park to the Great Salt Lake, Utah is a land of contrasts. It has five national parks, six national monuments, two national recreation areas, and one national historic site. The annual Railroader's Festival commemorating the meeting of the first transcontinental railroad is held at the Golden Spike National Historic Site. The Great Salt Lake is the largest lake west of the Mississippi with a salt content eight times that of the ocean. The Fossil Bone Quarry of Dinosaurs National Monument area displays hundreds of dinosaur bones exposed in a wall of sandstone. The oil found in huge oil shale deposits became profitable during the oil shortage of the early 1970's. Most of Utah's copper, the state's most valuable mineral, is taken from a mammoth open-pit mine in

UTAH

The name for this quilt pattern is "Utah Star." It is totally unique and like the many geological formations of this state, very eye catching.

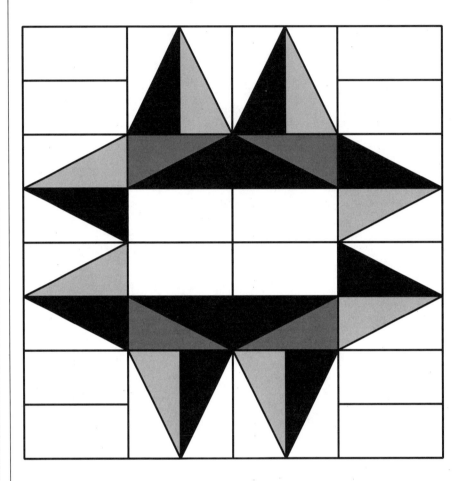

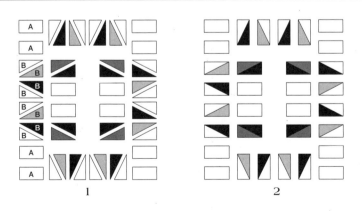

ASSEMBLY

Begin by laying out all the pieces in this arrangement (1). Sew B triangles to B triangles as shown in (2). Sew these pieced blocks together to make 4 blocks (2 at the top and two at the bottom) as in (3). Sew pieced and whole blocks together to make 4 strips (4), and sew these strips to each other to complete the "Utah Star" block (5).

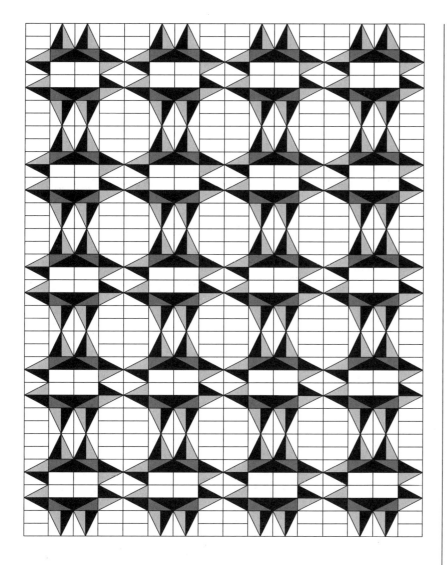

QUILT TOP

Placed side by side and top to bottom this unique design is achieved. The star is very outstanding in this arrangement. You could use sashing in between these blocks in this quilt top if you wish to experiment with dividing the stars from one another.

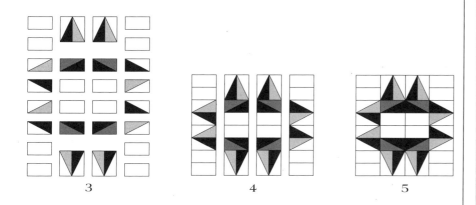

3   4   5

Bingham Canyon. People rushed to the Moab area in hopes of striking it rich when uranium was discovered here in 1952. Brigham Young's pioneer party came to the site of the current capital, Salt Lake City, in 1847. His restored home, Beehive House, is now a tourist attraction. Many travelers are drawn to this state by a mix of history and natural resources. Geological oddities from canyons to mountains compose spectacular scenery for all to enjoy.

- The sego lily, belonging to the tulip branch of the lily family, grows from an underground corm. Early settlers used these corms as food when their supplies dwindled. It has a few blue-green slender leaves and its bloom, while white, may be tinged with yellow, green, or lilac. These plants grow in great masses in the desert and in the midst of sagebrush.

- The blue spruce is the state tree and grows profusely in the scenic mountain parks of Utah. Spruces grow straight and tall tapering to a point at the top. The blue spruce is a very popular ornamental because of its unique coloring.

- Oddly enough the state bird is the sea gull. Usually thought of as birds of the sea, they spend a good amount of time inland. Though native to California, it is credited with saving crops planted by early settlers in Utah from an onslaught of black crickets that plagued the area for three successive growing seasons. The gulls came, ate the crickets, and the crops were saved.

Utah pattern – page 158

VERMONT
The Green
Mountain State

Vermont was the 14th state admitted to the United States in 1791. Farming and tourism are very important in this small but scenic state. After the spectacular fall in this colorful mountainous state, snow-covered peaks attract skiers throughout the winter. Vermont marble has been used for many famous monuments and some of the world's most magnificent buildings. The Vermont Marble Exhibit in Proctor showcases this most enduring natural resource. Granite quarries supply the world's largest stone-finishing plant at Millstone Hill in Barre, the granite capital of the world. The sugar maple not only provides spectacular color in the fall, but also produces over 300,000 gallons of maple syrup each year from this state. At the New England Maple Museum in Pittsford you can observe the process of cooking and reducing 40 gallons of sap to make a single gallon of this dark amber syrup. Norman Rockwell

VERMONT

The name for this quilt pattern is "Vermont Star." This pattern makes a gorgeous quilt top and is an excellent choice to use scrap pieces.

1

2

ASSEMBLY

Begin by laying out all the pieces in this arrangement (1). Sew A pieces to A pieces as shown in (2). Sew these pieced blocks together to make strips as in (3). Sew these strips together (4), and sew B to strips to make corner triangles (5). Finally, sew these corner triangles to the center pieced strip to complete the "Vermont Star" block (6).

QUILT TOP

Placed side by side and top to bottom this wonderful design is achieved and fools the eye by forming another design where the corners meet. This traditional arrangement can be very effective with a carefully planned color scheme or with the use of various light-medium and dark scraps.

3   4   5

6

moved to Arlington, and it was there that he produced some of his most famous illustrations using the people of Vermont as his models. Today in an historic 1800's church in Arlington hundreds of his *Saturday Evening Post* illustrations can be seen. The Bennington Museum features the Grandma Moses Gallery, and the Vermont State Craft Center at Frog Hollow showcases the best handmade crafts in the state. The Shelburne Museum covers 45 acres near Lake Champlain, and is the home of 37 historic structures and more than 200,000 pieces of Americana. The Vermont Quilt Festival is held annually in early July in Northfield. This quilt event features exhibits, lectures, classes, vendors, and many other activities.

■ Vermont's state flower is red clover, which may grow up to 2 feet tall. The flower head of this ground cover is about one inch across and features leaves that go to sleep at night folding the top leaflet over the two side ones.

■ The state tree is, of course, the sugar maple. A fine shade and ornamental tree, it is most famous for the sap it produces. The leaves turn a rich yellow, orange, or scarlet in the fall. The wood is excellent for furniture, cabinetry, and wood turnings.

■ The state bird is the hermit thrush. This shy bird has a distinctly reddish-brown tail, light under-breast with chains of brown-black markings on his throat and breast, and a buff-colored eye-ring.

Vermont pattern – page 159

VIRGINIA
The Mother of Presidents

Virginia was the 10th state admitted to the United States in 1788. This state gained its nickname because eight presidents were born here: George Washington, Thomas Jefferson, James Madison, James Monroe, William Henry Harrison, John Tyler, Zachory Taylor, and Woodrow Wilson. Because it is one of the 13 original colonies it is full to overflowing with history. Settlers first came to Jamestown in 1607. Now there are reproductions of the old James Fort and the ships that brought the settlers at the Jamestown Settlers Park. After the battle of Yorktown, Cornwallis surrendered to Washington, ending the Revolutionary War. General Lee surrendered to General Grant at the close of the Civil War at Appomattox Court House. Across the Potomac from Washington, D.C., is the home of one of the most recognizable American monuments, the Iwo Jima Marine Corps Memorial. Tobacco is a valuable resource for this state. While a small percentage of land is actually used in

VIRGINIA

The name for this quilt pattern is "Virginia Reel." You can do amazing designs with this block. It is not difficult to construct and the results are very striking. Be sure to experiment with many different materials divided into dark and light categories and you won't be disappointed with the results.

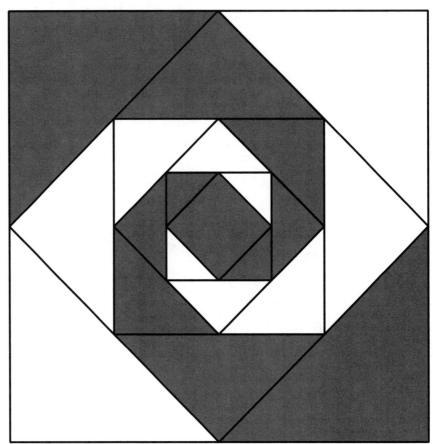

1   2

ASSEMBLY

Begin by laying out all the pieces in this arrangement (1). Sew C pieces to center square D (2). Attach E triangles to CD square (3). Sew B to ECD square (4), and sew F to BECD square (5), and finally sew A corners to FBECD to complete the "Virginia Reel" block (6).

QUILT TOP

Place side by side but drop each block by 6" vertically to stagger the assembly of this quilt to achieve this design. This arrangement really gives the feeling of movement diagonally across this quilt top.

3

4

5

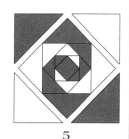

6

tobacco production, more farm income is generated by tobacco than any other crop. In the capital of Richmond, the National Tobacco Festival is held every year during the first two weeks in October. Coal is the most abundant natural mineral resource with most of it being found in the southwestern area of the state. There are many tourist attractions in addition to the historic sights. The skyline drive in the Blue Ridge Mountains is beautiful in almost any season, and the Atlantic Ocean coastline and Chesapeake Bay offer many popular watersports.

■ Virginia's state flower and tree is the flowering dogwood. The bark and leaves of the European species were brewed to make a lotion to treat mange in dogs. Perhaps the tree's name developed from this practice. The flowers of this slow-growing tree blossom in early spring. Red berries develop when the flowers drop away. Because the wood of this tree is so dense and fine-grained, it is unequaled for making shuttles for weaving.

■ West Virginia, Illinois, Indiana, Kentucky, North Carolina, Ohio, and Virginia share the cardinal as state bird. This brilliant red bird is the outstanding member of the sparrow family. Cardinals are a favorite at domestic birdfeeders.

Virginia pattern – page 160

BYE AND BYE

WASHINGTON
The Evergreen State

Washington was the 42nd state admitted to the United States in 1889. It is the only state named in honor of a president. A state of great beauty and contrast, it is bordered by the Pacific Ocean to the west and Canada to the north. It has large areas of thick evergreen forests, high mountains, the Olympic Peninsula jungle-like forests (one of the rainiest places in the world), and semi-desert lands in the southeast. Nicknamed the "Evergreen State," vast amounts of trees provide lumber, pulp, paper, and an endless amount of wood products. The apple is an important agricultural export. Washington produces more apples than any other state and doubles its closest competitor – New York. The fishing industry thrives here because of the Pacific Ocean coastline and the numerous bays, inlets, rivers, and lakes throughout the state. Grand Coulee Dam, the largest concrete dam in the U.S. located on the Columbia River, is one of the engineering marvels of the world. The Boeing Com-

WASHINGTON

The name for this quilt pattern is "Washington Pavement." It is reminiscent of a pineapple design and is an easy but striking block to make.

ASSEMBLY

Begin by laying out all the pieces in this arrangement (1). Sew E pieces to center D square (2). Attach C to ED section (3). Sew F to CED section (4), and sew B to FCED section (5). Sew G to BFCED section (6). Attach the A corners to complete this "Washington Pavement" block (7).

QUILT TOP

Placed side by side and top to bottom, the "Washington Pavement" block makes a quilt that will create this design. You may want to put sashing in between these blocks to separate them so that the individual block will be easier to see.

4

5

6

7

pany, headquartered in Seattle, is a leading producer of aircraft and spacecraft, and the Hanford Project of Energy Research and Development Administration located near Richland brought Washington into the nuclear age. Since the 1962 World's Fair, the most recognizable building associated with Washington state would have to be the Space Needle in Seattle.

■ The early summer flowers of the coast rhododendron, Washington's state flower, nearly cover the bush. It grows 20 feet in height, and remains a shrub as opposed to the mountain rhododendron of West Virginia which is a tree that grows almost twice as tall.

■ Western hemlock is the state's tree. This evergreen will grow to an amazing height of 100 feet. They are easily transplanted when small. Because of their beauty and hardy nature they are widely used in ornamental hedges.

■ The willow goldfinch is Washington's state bird. It is smaller than a sparrow with a bright yellow body, black wings, tail, and cap. It is nicknamed a "wild canary" because of its size and color.

Washington pattern – page 162

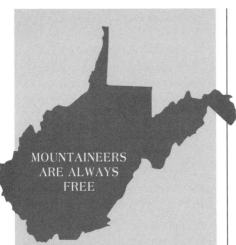

WEST VIRGINIA
The Mountain State

West Virginia was the 35th state admitted to the United States in 1863. This state broke apart form Virginia at the beginning of the Civil War by refusing to secede from the Union. As you might guess from this state's nickname, "the Mountain State," there is very little flat land here. Though relatively small in size this state has a great variety of natural resources, such as timber, minerals, abundant rainfall, wildlife, and tourism attractions. The extremely rugged terrain does not allow for much agriculture, but the beauty of it, and the natural mineral springs and ski slopes found here, bring in many tourists. The largest money producing mineral is undoubtedly coal. Deposits of this black fuel lie under more than half the state. A tragic coal mine explosion and fire at Farmington in 1968 led Congress to pass stronger laws regulating mine safety and working conditions. Skill

WEST VIRGINIA

The name for this quilt pattern is "West Virginia." This pattern can be made to make the center star stand out or to give a very overall dimensional theme. Try experimenting with coloring this design in several ways before beginning your project.

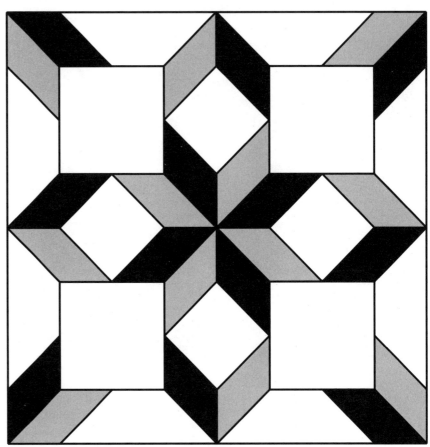

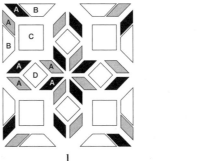

1   2

ASSEMBLY

Begin by laying out all the pieces in this arrangement (1). Sew A pieces to B pieces and medium A pieces to dark A pieces as shown (2). Attach 1 AB section to each C square and AA sections to D squares (3). Attach remaining AB sections to ABC sections. Sew 2 AAD sections together (4), and then sew these attached AAD sections together making the center (5). Attach corners to complete the West Virginia star (6).

QUILT TOP

The West Virginia block is a beautiful and traditional design when placed side by side and top to bottom. By experimenting with your colors you can make the stars formed by the center and corners of this block stand out.

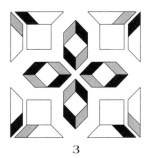

3

4

5

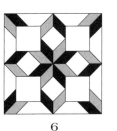

6

in handcrafts is an art handed down from generation to generation here. Weaving and quiltmaking have always been a necessary and now popular art in this mountainous country.

- The state flower is the rhododendron. This mountain species grows to be as tall as 35 feet. The blossom, usually rose colored, grows in clusters at the end of the branches. Its glossy dark green leaves will droop in freezing weather, but the plant will thrive in the cold. The sight of these beautiful blossoms covering the mountainsides in the spring in West Virginia is a special treat.

- The sugar maple is the state's tree. The beautiful color ranges of its leaves from season to season is partly responsible for the outstanding beauty of the West Virginia mountains.

- Favored by more states than any bird, the brilliant cardinal is West Virginia's state bird along with Illinois, Indiana, Kentucky, North Carolina, Ohio, and Virginia.

West Virginia pattern – page 164

WISCONSIN

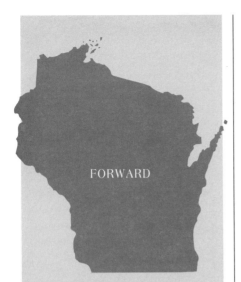

WISCONSIN
The Badger State

Wisconsin was the 30th state admitted to the United States in 1848. The Republican Party was formed in this Midwestern state. It has more than 8,000 lakes and borders on Lake Superior and Lake Michigan to the north and east, and the Mississippi river to the west. These features give this state wonderful natural beauty and attract millions of visitors each year. In fact, tourism now ranks as the second highest revenue producer. The Wisconsin Dells, a seven mile long canyon cut and carved by the Wisconsin River, is a popular tourist attraction. Manufacturing and agriculture are also strong revenue producers. Wisconsin farmers help fill the nation's dinner tables with green peas, beets, cabbage, sweet corn, cranberries, and, of course, milk. The World Dairy Exposition is held each October in the capital of Madison. In 1973 the Wisconsin Arts Board was formed to

The name for this quilt pattern is "Wisconsin Star." It has seven basic pattern pieces that center on an octagon piece.

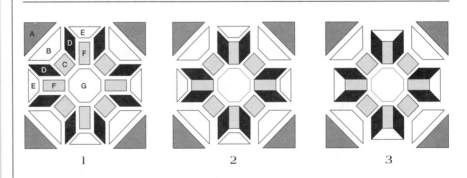

1   2   3

ASSEMBLY

While this assembly looks strange, if you take it one step at a time it will be easy. Begin by laying out all the pieces in this arrangement (1). Piece the 8 D dark pieces to the sides of the medium-light F rectangles (2). Next sew light E pieces into the DF pieced portions (3), sew the corner medium A pieces to the light B pieces and the medium-light C squares to the center G octagon (4). Then sew the pieced DEF sections to the pieced CG section (5). To make your Wisconsin Star block complete sew the AB section into each corner (6).

QUILT TOP

The "Wisconsin Star" is a very direct pattern and makes a fine traditionally clear design when placed side by side and top to bottom.

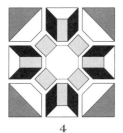

4

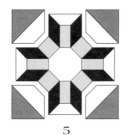

5

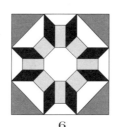

6

encourage and support artistic endeavors throughout this state. They produce an Arts and Craft Fairs Directory that you may have free of charge by writing to the Wisconsin Arts Board.

■ The state flower is the bird's foot or wood violet. The leaves of this wild violet are not the large heart shape most of us are used to seeing. They are more slender and roughly shaped like a bird's foot, thus the name! The flower is two toned – light and dark purple. As the flowers fade, the foliage takes over for the summer months. These violets are a lovely perennial.

■ As with West Virginia, Vermont, and New York, the sugar maple is Wisconsin's state tree.

■ Michigan and Connecticut share the robin with Wisconsin as the state bird.

Wisconsin pattern – page 165

WYOMING The Equality State

Wyoming was the 44th state admitted to the United States in 1890. It is the home of Yellowstone National Park, the first of our country's national parks. This state has some of the most beautiful scenery found anywhere. Devil's Tower National Monument is a most recognizable natural volcanic formation. Cheyenne, the capital of this state, has hosted the Frontier Days annual celebration every year during the last week in July since 1897. This state is rich in museums, most featuring pioneer and Native American cultures. The current economic base is largely supported by mining, and especially by the production of oil from over 7,600 wells in this state. The Rocky, Laramie, and Big Horn Mountains are found here along with a portion of the Great Plains and Black Hills. All these wonderfully western names and places make you think of Wyoming as being the rugged wild west. But this state was brought into the space age in 1960

WYOMING

The name for this quilt pattern is "Wyoming Valley." While this pattern looks complicated, with only three basic pattern pieces, it is easy to assemble.

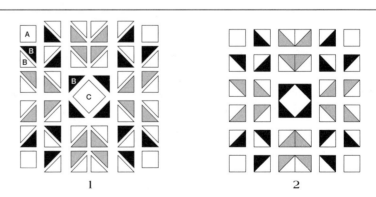

ASSEMBLY

This is another easy-to-assemble block. Begin by laying out all the pieces in this arrangement (1). Piece B half-squares together and sew B pieced squares together at the center. Sew B triangles to center C square (2). Sew these pieced squares together making five strips (3). Then, matching seams, sew these strips together to make the "Wyoming Valley" block (4).

QUILT TOP

When this "Wyoming Valley" block is placed side by side and top to bottom it becomes a pattern that fools the eye with its secondary design.

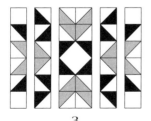

3

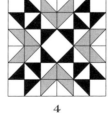

4

with the opening of the first operational intercontinental ballistic missile base near Cheyenne.

- The state flower is the Indian paintbrush. This seems only natural since Wyoming is steeped in Native American culture. This plant, a member of the figwart family, is wildly colorful with flowers of red and bright orange blossoming in the early summer.

- As with Kansas and Nebraska, the cottonwood is the state's tree. This group of trees, though short-lived, grow quickly and make excellent shade. Oil is made from its seeds and the hulls are put to use as food for livestock.

- The state bird is the meadowlark. With a distinctive black V marking on its yellow breast, this bird thrives on the grains from Wyoming's vast meadowlands. This bird is a wonderful songbird and valued as a natural controller of harmful insects.

Wyoming pattern – page 167

ALABAMA Pattern Pieces

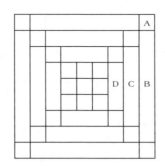

To make this block cut 17 dark color & 4 light color squares from pattern A, 4 medium color pieces from pattern B, 4 light color pieces from pattern C and 4 medium color pieces from pattern D.

A

CUT
17 DARK
&
4 LIGHT PER BLOCK

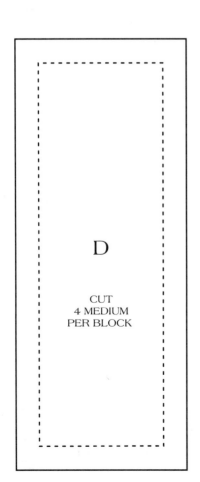

D

CUT
4 MEDIUM
PER BLOCK

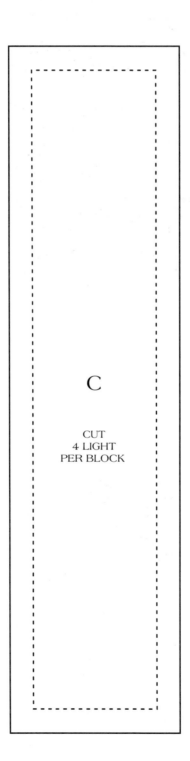

C

CUT
4 LIGHT
PER BLOCK

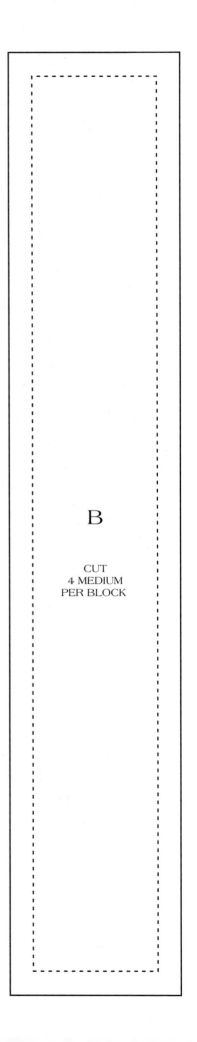

B

CUT
4 MEDIUM
PER BLOCK

ALASKA Pattern Pieces

To make this block cut 4 medium color pieces from pattern A, reverse the pattern and cut 4 more medium color pieces from pattern A. From pattern B cut 8 dark color triangles per block. From C cut 4 light color squares per block. Cut 4 light and 4 dark color triangles from pattern D. From E cut 4 medium color squares and from F cut 2 light and 2 dark triangles per block.

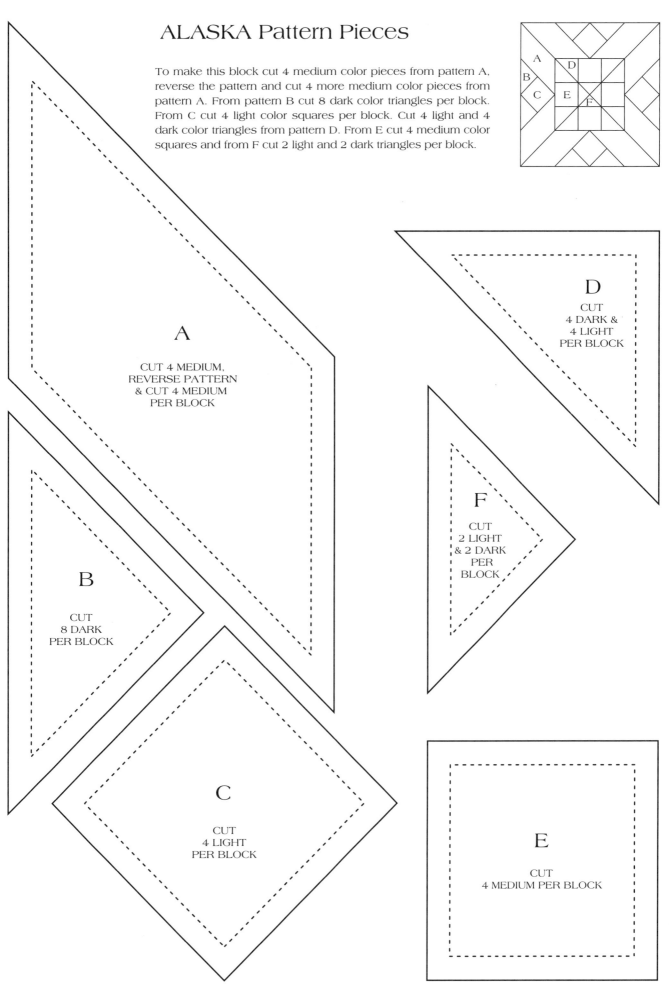

A

CUT 4 MEDIUM,
REVERSE PATTERN
& CUT 4 MEDIUM
PER BLOCK

D

CUT
4 DARK &
4 LIGHT
PER BLOCK

F

CUT
2 LIGHT
& 2 DARK
PER
BLOCK

B

CUT
8 DARK
PER BLOCK

C

CUT
4 LIGHT
PER BLOCK

E

CUT
4 MEDIUM PER BLOCK

ARIZONA Pattern Pieces

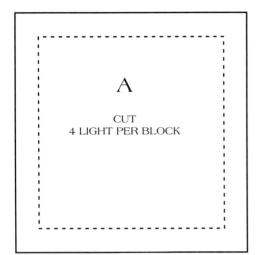

A
CUT
4 LIGHT PER BLOCK

To make this block cut 4 light color squares from pattern A. From pattern B cut 20 dark and 20 light color triangles per block. From C cut 4 light color rectangles per block. Cut 1 dark color square from pattern D.

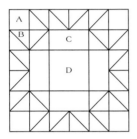

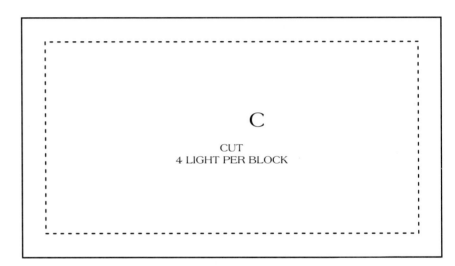

C
CUT
4 LIGHT PER BLOCK

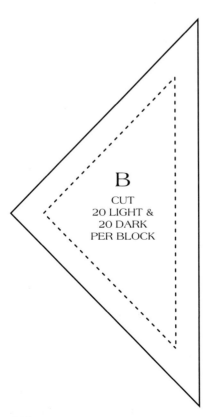

B
CUT
20 LIGHT &
20 DARK
PER BLOCK

D
CUT
1 DARK PER BLOCK

ARKANSAS Pattern Pieces

To make this block cut 5 light color squares from pattern A. From pattern B cut 4 medium-dark color rectangles per block. From C cut 4 medium color pieces per block. Cut 4 light color pieces from the D rectangle and from the E square cut 4 medium per block. Finally, from F cut 16 dark color triangles and from G cut 4 light color pieces, reverse and cut 4 more light color pieces per block.

B

CUT
4 MEDIUM-DARK
PER BLOCK

G

CUT 4 LIGHT,
REVERSE &
CUT 4 MORE
LIGHT PER
BLOCK

C

CUT
4 MEDIUM
PER BLOCK

E

CUT 4
MEDIUM
PER BLOCK

D

CUT
4 LIGHT
PER BLOCK

A

CUT
5 LIGHT
PER BLOCK

F

CUT 16
DARK
PER
BLOCK

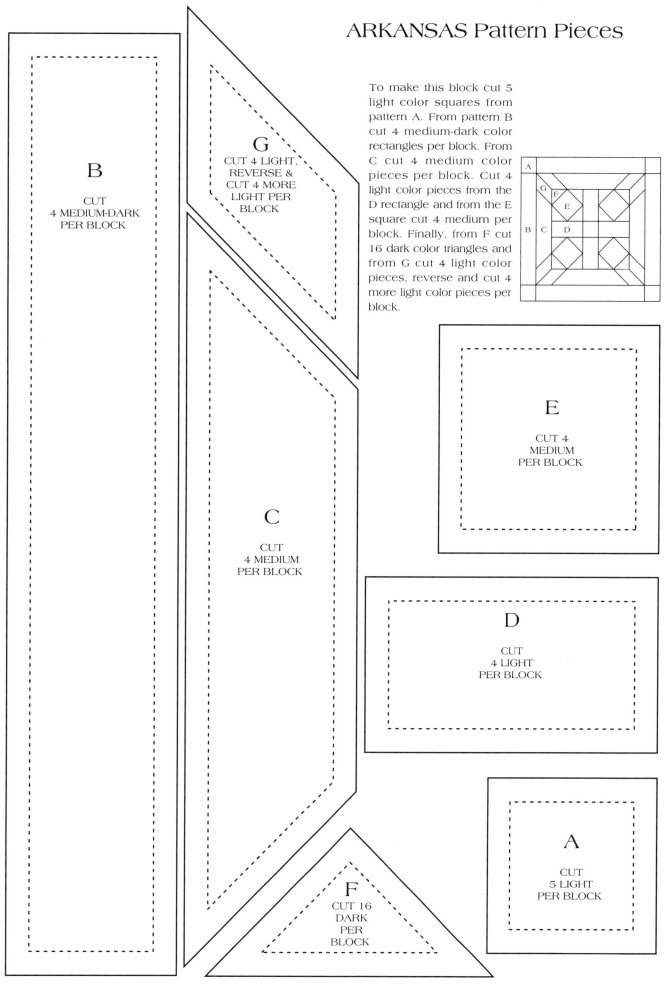

CALIFORNIA Pattern Pieces

To make this block cut 4 light color pieces from pattern A. From pattern B cut 4 medium color pieces per block. From C cut 4 light and 1 dark color square per block.

A
CUT 4 LIGHT PER BLOCK

C
CUT 1 DARK & 4 LIGHT PER BLOCK

B
CUT 4 MEDIUM PER BLOCK

COLORADO Pattern Pieces

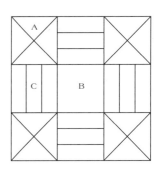

To make this block cut 8 dark and 8 light color triangles from pattern A. From square B cut 1 light color piece per block. From C cut 4 light and 8 dark color rectangles.

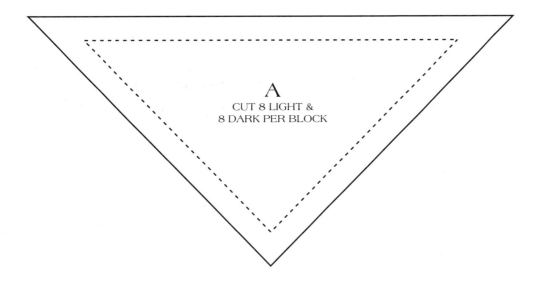

A
CUT 8 LIGHT & 8 DARK PER BLOCK

B
CUT 1 LIGHT PER BLOCK

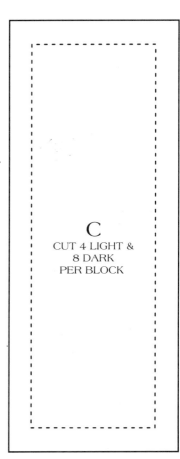

C
CUT 4 LIGHT & 8 DARK PER BLOCK

CONNECTICUT Pattern Pieces

To make this block cut 16 dark and 16 light color triangles from pattern A for each block.

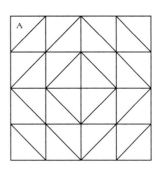

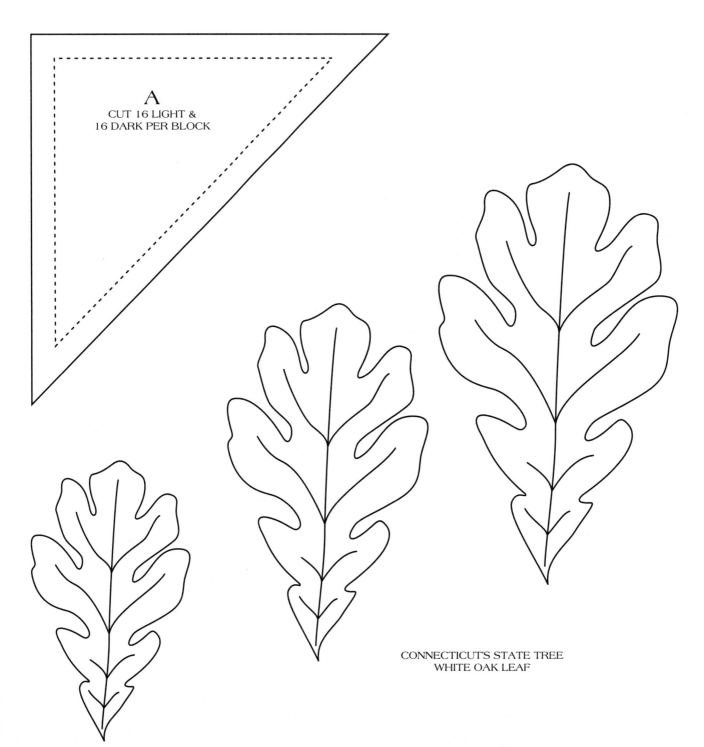

A
CUT 16 LIGHT &
16 DARK PER BLOCK

CONNECTICUT'S STATE TREE
WHITE OAK LEAF

DELAWARE Pattern Pieces

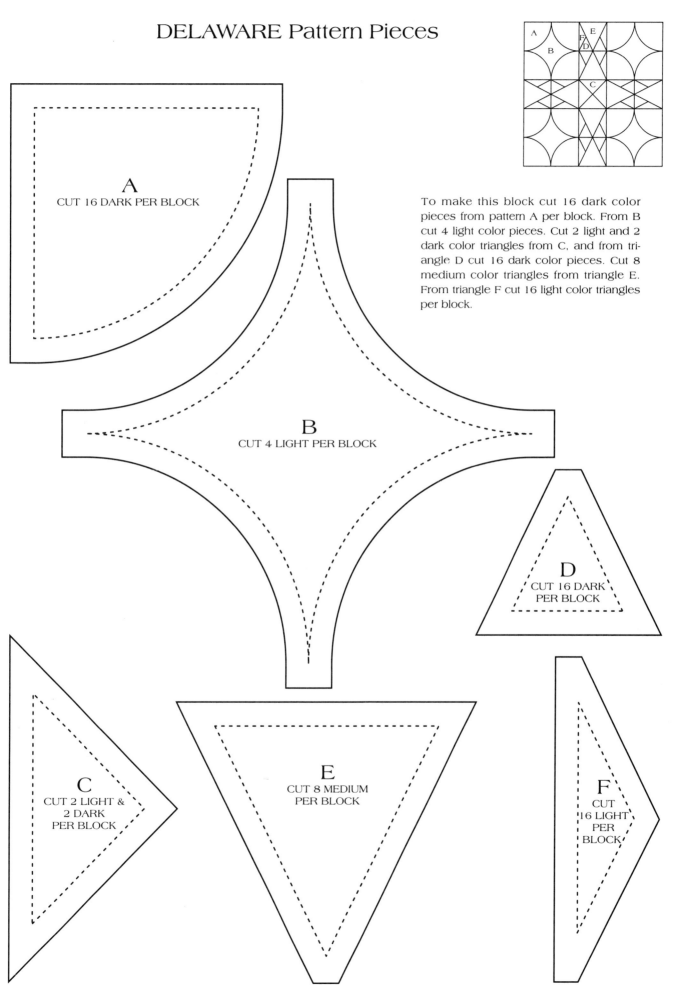

A
CUT 16 DARK PER BLOCK

B
CUT 4 LIGHT PER BLOCK

D
CUT 16 DARK
PER BLOCK

C
CUT 2 LIGHT &
2 DARK
PER BLOCK

E
CUT 8 MEDIUM
PER BLOCK

F
CUT
16 LIGHT
PER
BLOCK

To make this block cut 16 dark color pieces from pattern A per block. From B cut 4 light color pieces. Cut 2 light and 2 dark color triangles from C, and from triangle D cut 16 dark color pieces. Cut 8 medium color triangles from triangle E. From triangle F cut 16 light color triangles per block.

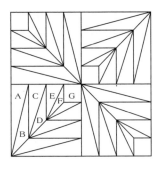

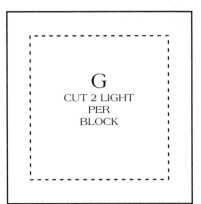

G
CUT 2 LIGHT
PER
BLOCK

FLORIDA Pattern Pieces

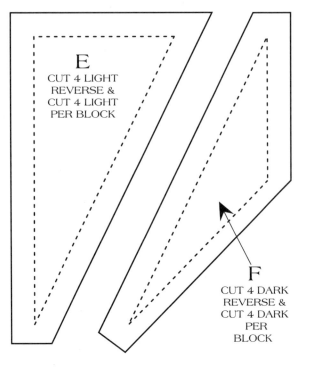

E
CUT 4 LIGHT
REVERSE &
CUT 4 LIGHT
PER BLOCK

F
CUT 4 DARK
REVERSE &
CUT 4 DARK
PER
BLOCK

To make this block from A cut 4 light color triangles, reverse and cut 4 more light color triangles per block. From B cut 4 dark color triangles, reverse and cut 4 more dark color triangles. Cut 4 light color triangles, reverse and cut 4 more light color triangles from C for each block. From D cut 4 dark color triangles, reverse and cut 4 more dark color triangles. Cut 4 light color triangles, reverse and cut 4 more light color triangles from E. From F cut 4 dark color triangles, reverse and cut 4 more dark color triangles. And finally from G cut 2 light color squares.

A
CUT 4 LIGHT
REVERSE &
CUT 4 LIGHT
PER BLOCK

B
CUT 4 DARK
REVERSE &
CUT 4 DARK
PER BLOCK

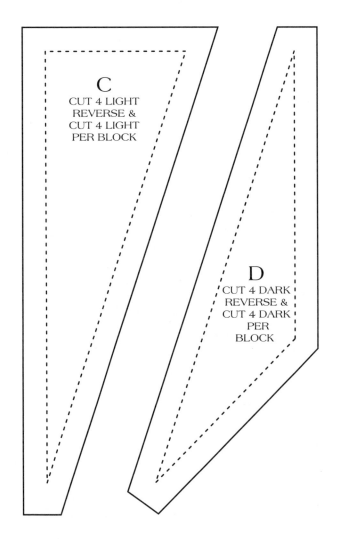

C
CUT 4 LIGHT
REVERSE &
CUT 4 LIGHT
PER BLOCK

D
CUT 4 DARK
REVERSE &
CUT 4 DARK
PER
BLOCK

GEORGIA Pattern Pieces

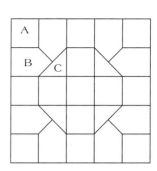

To make this block cut 8 light, 4 dark, and 1 medium color squares from pattern A. From B cut 8 medium color pieces, and from C cut 4 dark triangles for each block.

B
CUT
8 MEDIUM
PER BLOCK

C
CUT
4 DARK
PER BLOCK

A
CUT
8 LIGHT,
4 DARK &
1 MEDIUM
PER BLOCK

GEORGIA CHEROKEE ROSE

HAWAII Pattern Pieces

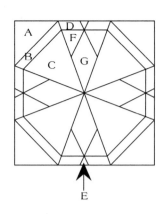

To make this block cut 4 dark color triangles from pattern A. From B cut 4 light color pieces per block. Cut 4 medium color triangles from pattern C. With pattern D you will need to cut 4 light color pieces, reverse the pattern and cut 4 more light color pieces. Cut 4 dark color triangles from pattern E. From pattern F cut 4 light color triangles, reverse the pattern and cut 4 more light color triangles. Finally from pattern G cut 4 dark diamonds per block.

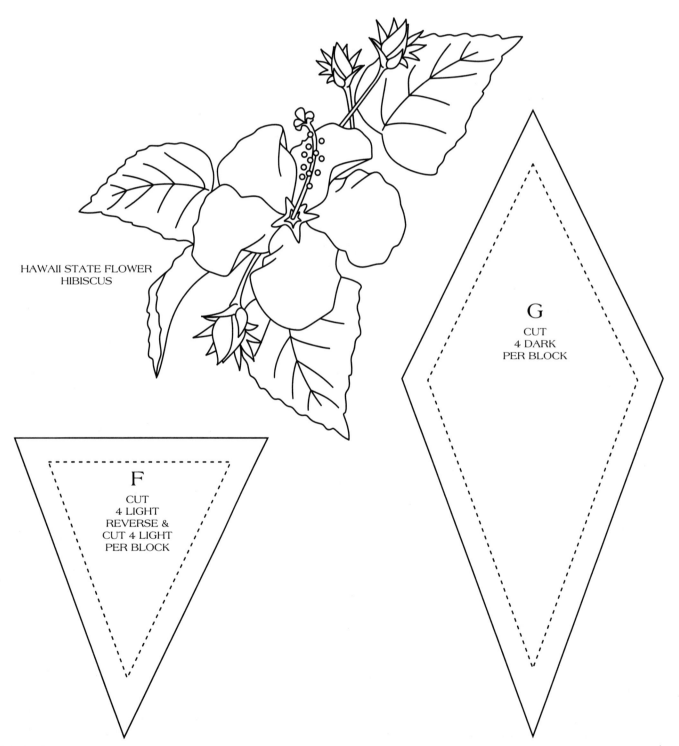

HAWAII STATE FLOWER
HIBISCUS

G
CUT
4 DARK
PER BLOCK

F
CUT
4 LIGHT
REVERSE &
CUT 4 LIGHT
PER BLOCK

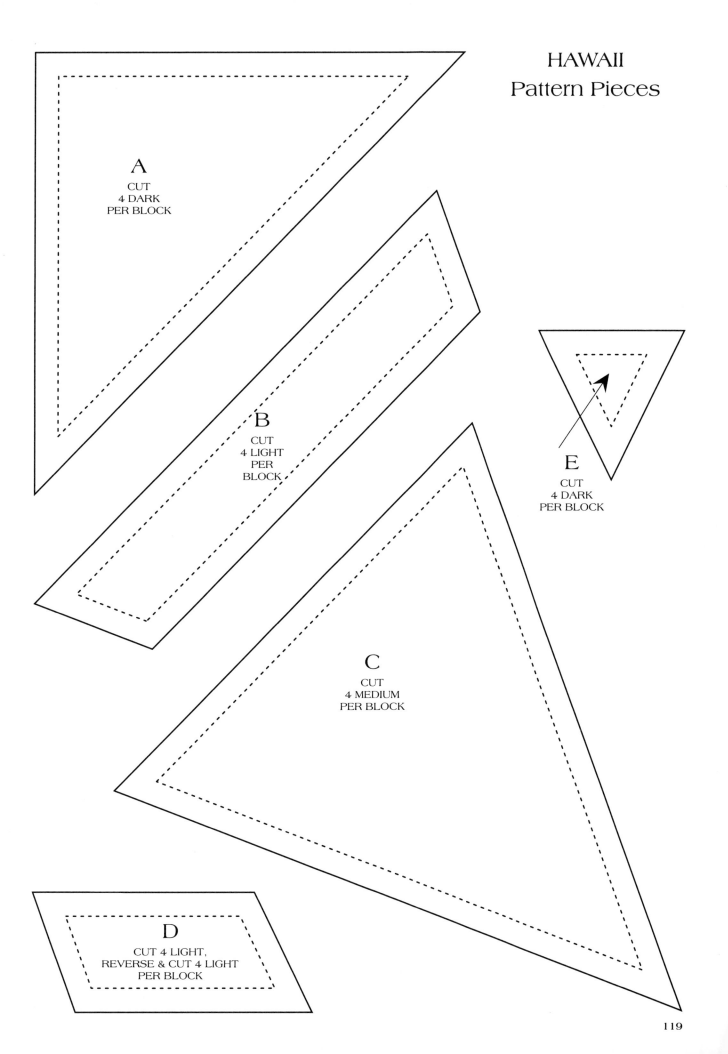

HAWAII
Pattern Pieces

A
CUT
4 DARK
PER BLOCK

B
CUT
4 LIGHT
PER
BLOCK

C
CUT
4 MEDIUM
PER BLOCK

D
CUT 4 LIGHT,
REVERSE & CUT 4 LIGHT
PER BLOCK

E
CUT
4 DARK
PER BLOCK

119

IDAHO Pattern Pieces

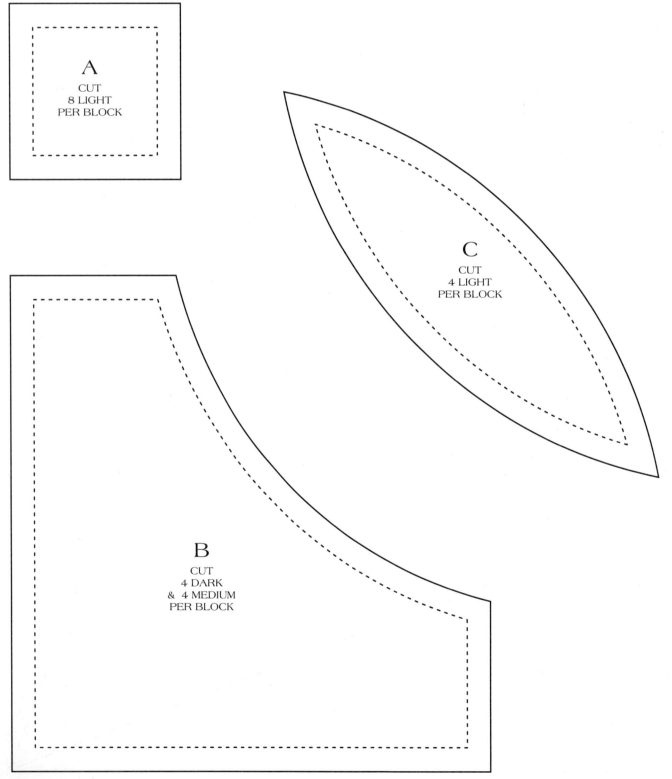

To make this block cut 8 light color squares from pattern A. Cut 4 dark and 4 medium color pieces from pattern B. From C cut 4 light color pieces per block.

A
CUT
8 LIGHT
PER BLOCK

C
CUT
4 LIGHT
PER BLOCK

B
CUT
4 DARK
& 4 MEDIUM
PER BLOCK

ILLINOIS Pattern Pieces

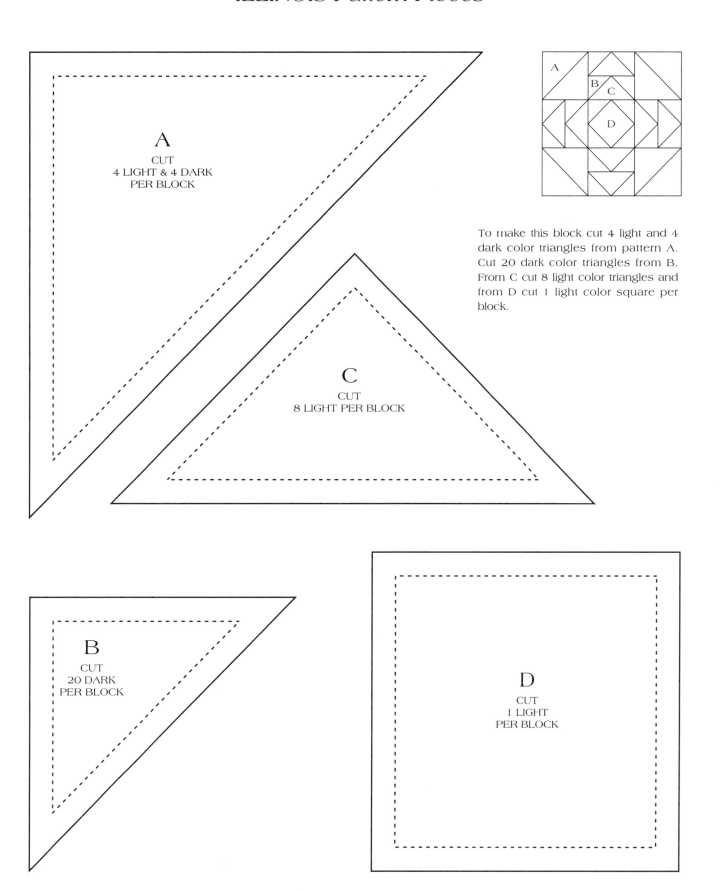

A
CUT
4 LIGHT & 4 DARK
PER BLOCK

C
CUT
8 LIGHT PER BLOCK

B
CUT
20 DARK
PER BLOCK

D
CUT
1 LIGHT
PER BLOCK

To make this block cut 4 light and 4 dark color triangles from pattern A. Cut 20 dark color triangles from B. From C cut 8 light color triangles and from D cut 1 light color square per block.

INDIANA Pattern Pieces

To make this block cut 4 dark color pieces from pattern A. Cut 4 light color pieces from B, reverse and cut 4 more light color pieces from this same pattern. From C cut 4 dark color pieces, from D cut 4 light color pieces, and from E cut only 1 dark color piece.

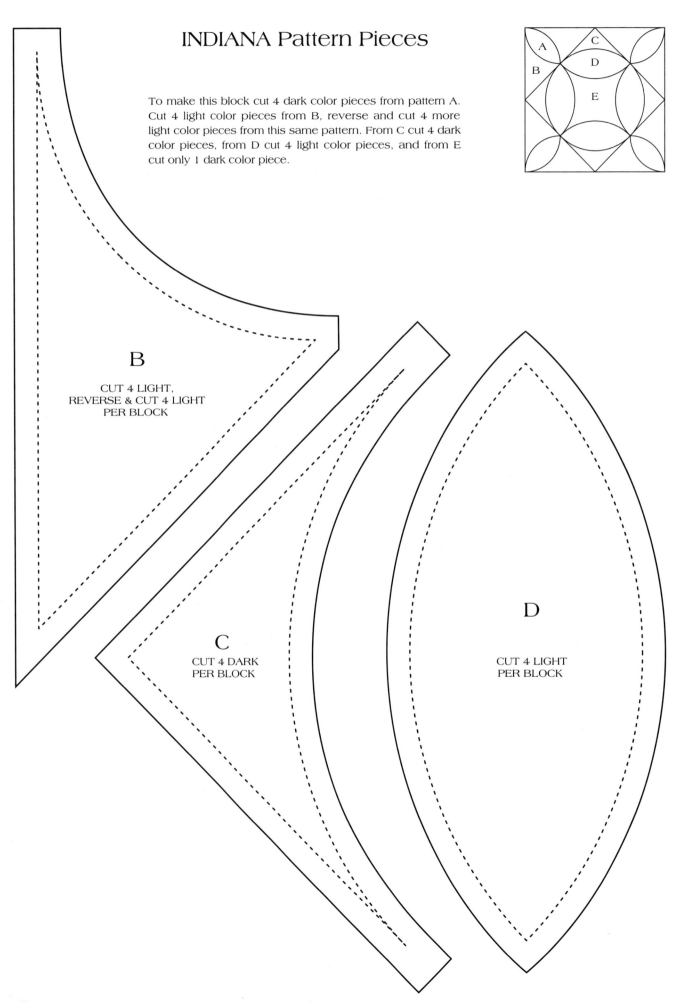

B

CUT 4 LIGHT,
REVERSE & CUT 4 LIGHT
PER BLOCK

C

CUT 4 DARK
PER BLOCK

D

CUT 4 LIGHT
PER BLOCK

INDIANA Pattern Pieces

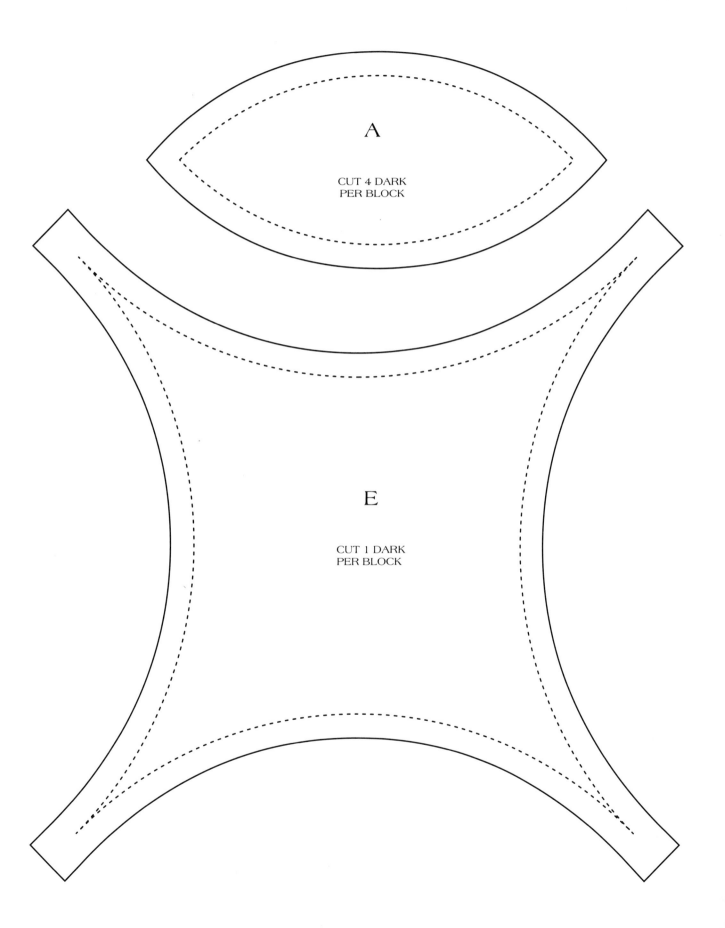

A

CUT 4 DARK
PER BLOCK

E

CUT 1 DARK
PER BLOCK

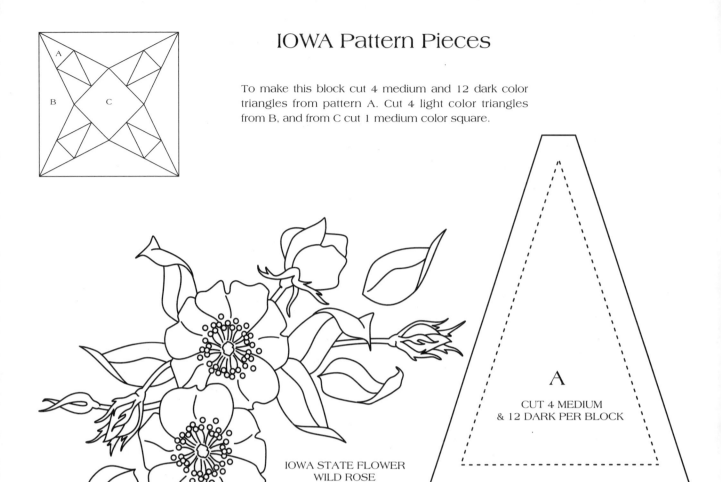

IOWA Pattern Pieces

To make this block cut 4 medium and 12 dark color triangles from pattern A. Cut 4 light color triangles from B, and from C cut 1 medium color square.

A

CUT 4 MEDIUM
& 12 DARK PER BLOCK

IOWA STATE FLOWER
WILD ROSE

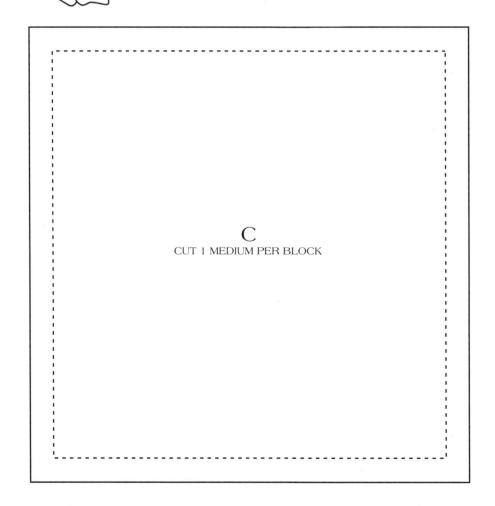

C

CUT 1 MEDIUM PER BLOCK

IOWA Pattern Pieces

B
CUT 4 LIGHT PER BLOCK

KANSAS Pattern Pieces

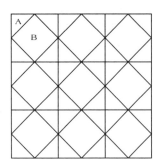

To make this block cut 16 dark and 20 light color triangles from pattern A. Cut 5 medium and 4 light color squares from B.

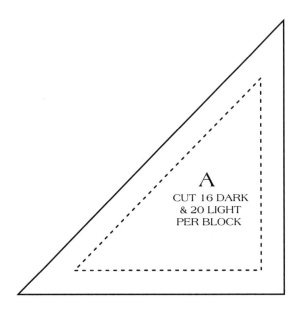

B
CUT 5 MEDIUM
& 4 LIGHT PER BLOCK

A
CUT 16 DARK
& 20 LIGHT
PER BLOCK

KANSAS STATE FLOWER
SUNFLOWER

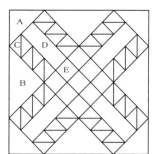

KENTUCKY Pattern Pieces

To make this block cut 4 medium color triangles from pattern A. Cut 4 medium color triangles from B. From C cut 24 dark and 24 light color triangles. Cut 4 light color rectangles from D and from pattern E cut 5 light and 4 dark squares.

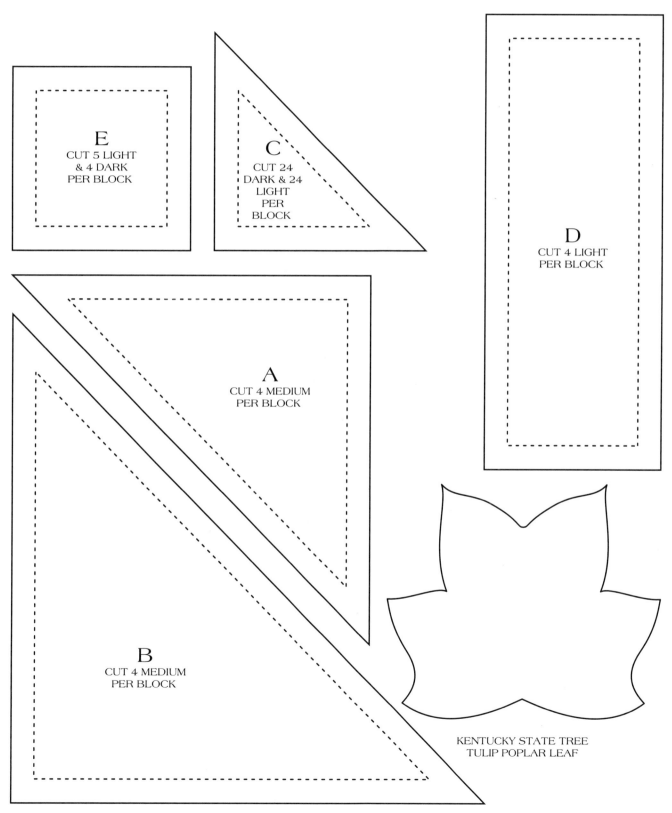

E
CUT 5 LIGHT
& 4 DARK
PER BLOCK

C
CUT 24
DARK & 24
LIGHT
PER
BLOCK

D
CUT 4 LIGHT
PER BLOCK

A
CUT 4 MEDIUM
PER BLOCK

B
CUT 4 MEDIUM
PER BLOCK

KENTUCKY STATE TREE
TULIP POPLAR LEAF

LOUISIANA Pattern Pieces

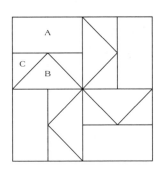

To make this block cut 4 light color rectangles from pattern A. Cut 4 dark color triangles from B, and from C cut 8 medium color triangles.

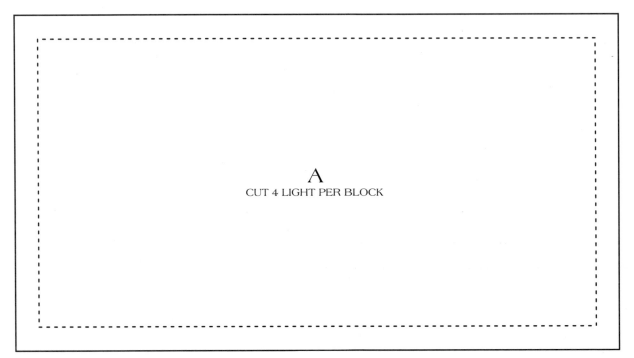

A
CUT 4 LIGHT PER BLOCK

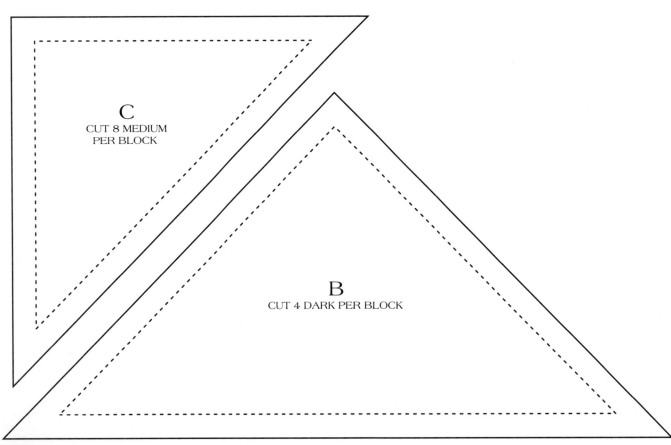

C
CUT 8 MEDIUM
PER BLOCK

B
CUT 4 DARK PER BLOCK

MAINE Pattern Pieces

To make this block cut 12 light and 12 dark color triangles from pattern A. Cut 8 light color triangles from B. From C cut 8 light color pieces. Cut 4 medium color pieces from pattern D. Cut 4 medium color pieces per block from pattern E. And finally from F cut 8 dark per block.

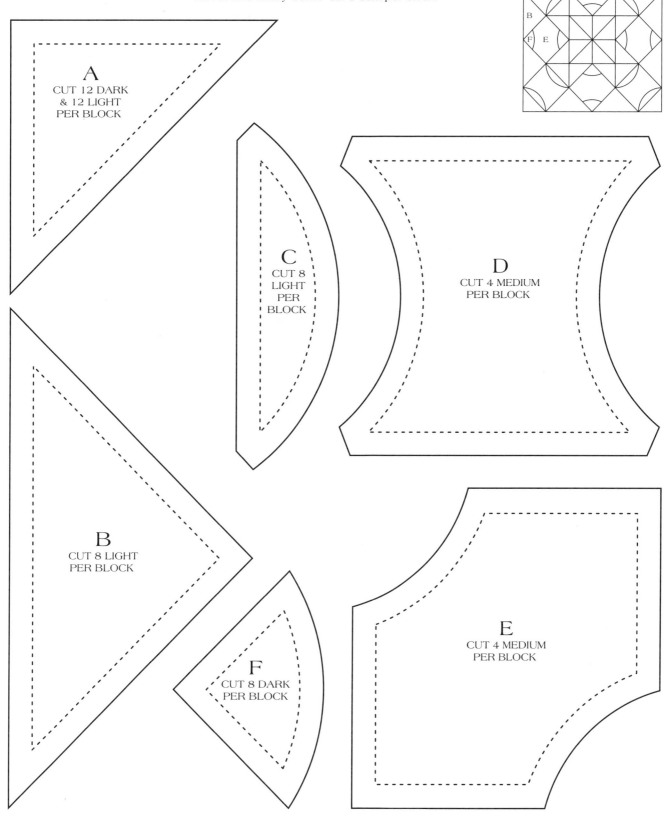

A
CUT 12 DARK
& 12 LIGHT
PER BLOCK

C
CUT 8
LIGHT
PER
BLOCK

D
CUT 4 MEDIUM
PER BLOCK

B
CUT 8 LIGHT
PER BLOCK

F
CUT 8 DARK
PER BLOCK

E
CUT 4 MEDIUM
PER BLOCK

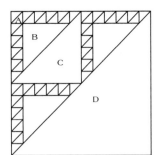

MARYLAND Pattern Pieces

To make this block cut 27 dark and 33 light color triangles from pattern A. Cut 3 medium color triangles from B and from C cut 1 light color triangle. Cut 1 large light color triangle from pattern D.

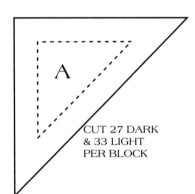

A

CUT 27 DARK & 33 LIGHT PER BLOCK

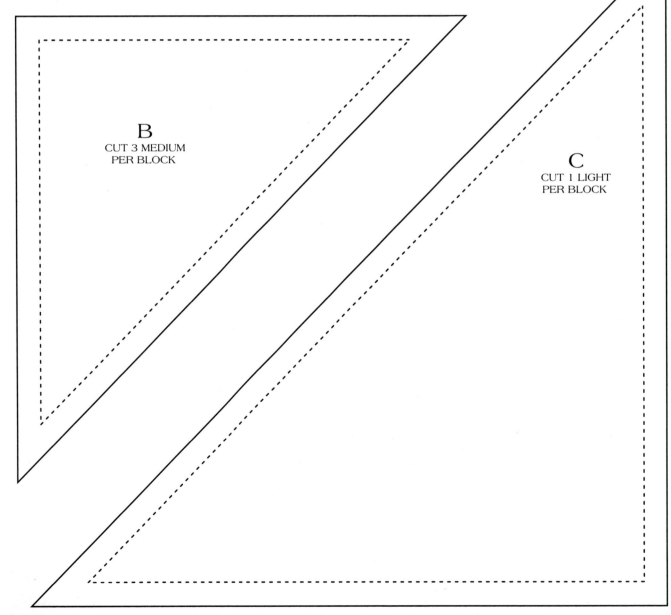

B
CUT 3 MEDIUM PER BLOCK

C
CUT 1 LIGHT PER BLOCK

MARYLAND Pattern Pieces

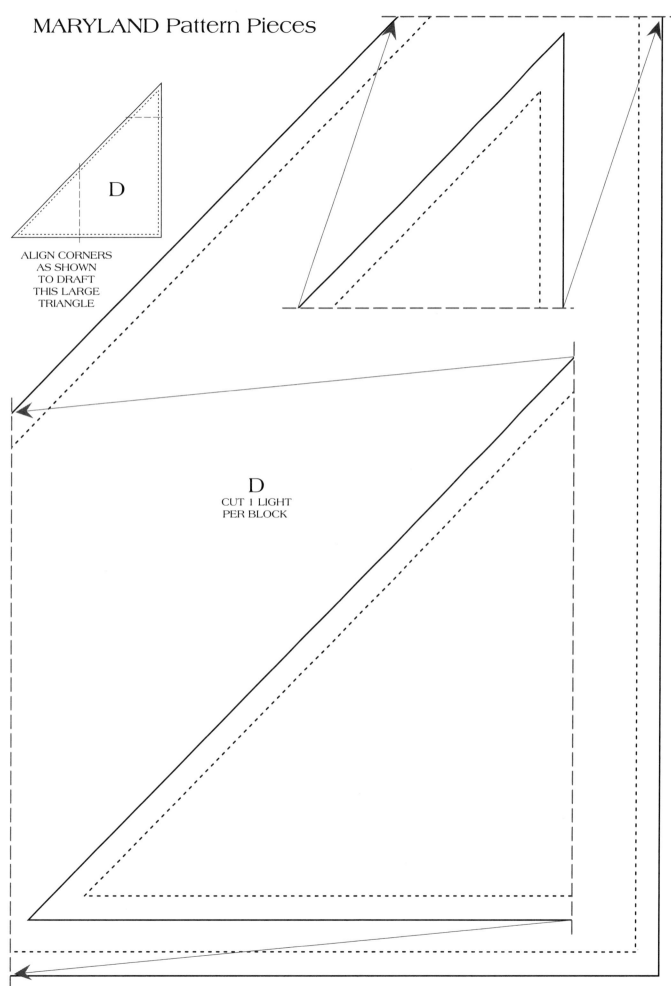

D

ALIGN CORNERS
AS SHOWN
TO DRAFT
THIS LARGE
TRIANGLE

D

CUT 1 LIGHT
PER BLOCK

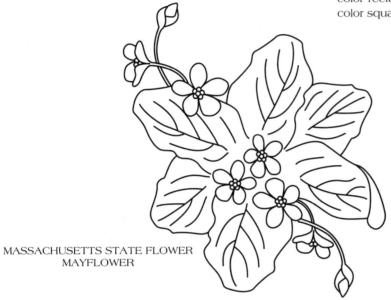

MASSACHUSETTS Pattern Pieces

To make this block cut 4 light and 4 dark color squares from pattern A. Cut 56 light and 56 dark color triangles from B. From C cut 2 medium-light color rectangles. Cut 2 light and 2 medium-light color rectangles from D, 2 light color rectangles from pattern E, and 1 medium color square from pattern F.

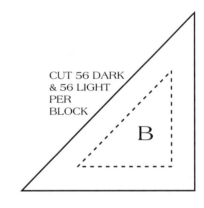

CUT 56 DARK
& 56 LIGHT
PER
BLOCK

B

MASSACHUSETTS STATE FLOWER
MAYFLOWER

A
CUT 4 DARK
& 4 LIGHT
PER BLOCK

F
CUT 1 MEDIUM
PER BLOCK

MASSACHUSETTS Pattern Pieces

C
CUT 2
MEDIUM-LIGHT
PER BLOCK

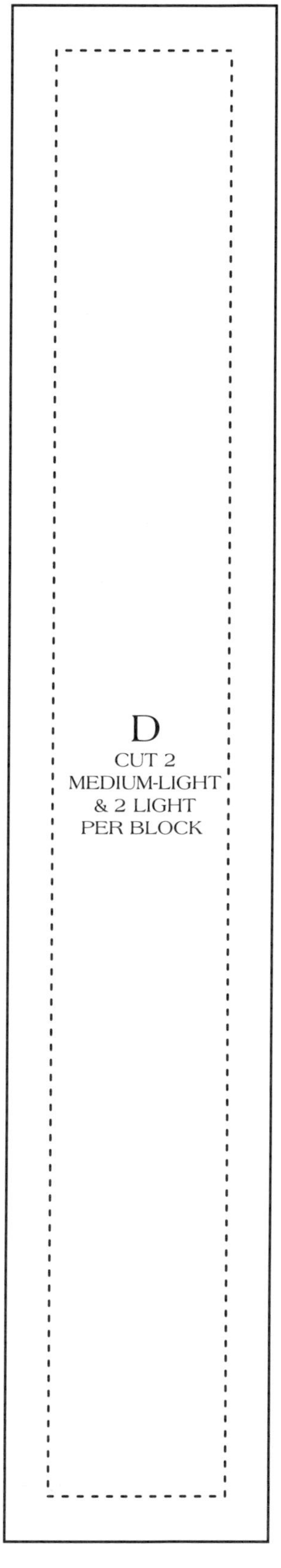

D
CUT 2
MEDIUM-LIGHT
& 2 LIGHT
PER BLOCK

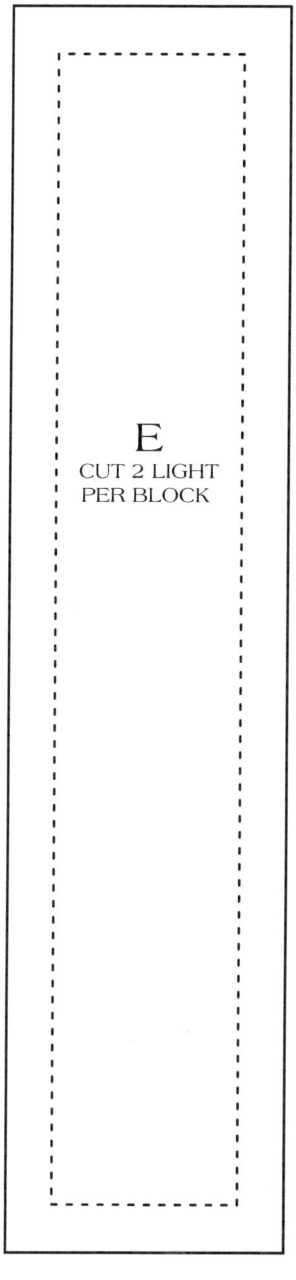

E
CUT 2 LIGHT
PER BLOCK

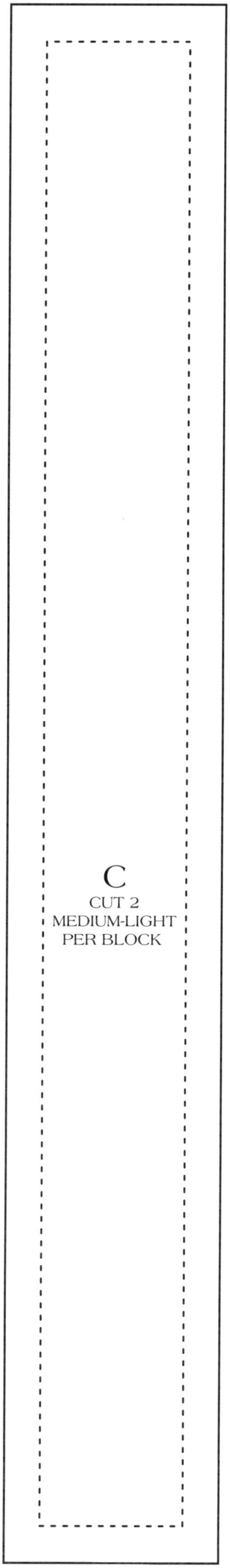

MICHIGAN Pattern Pieces

To make this block cut 4 light squares from pattern A. Cut 8 light color triangles from B. From C cut 4 medium color pieces, reverse C and cut 4 more medium color pieces. Also cut 4 dark pieces from C, reverse and cut 4 more dark pieces from pattern C. Cut 1 light square from pattern D.

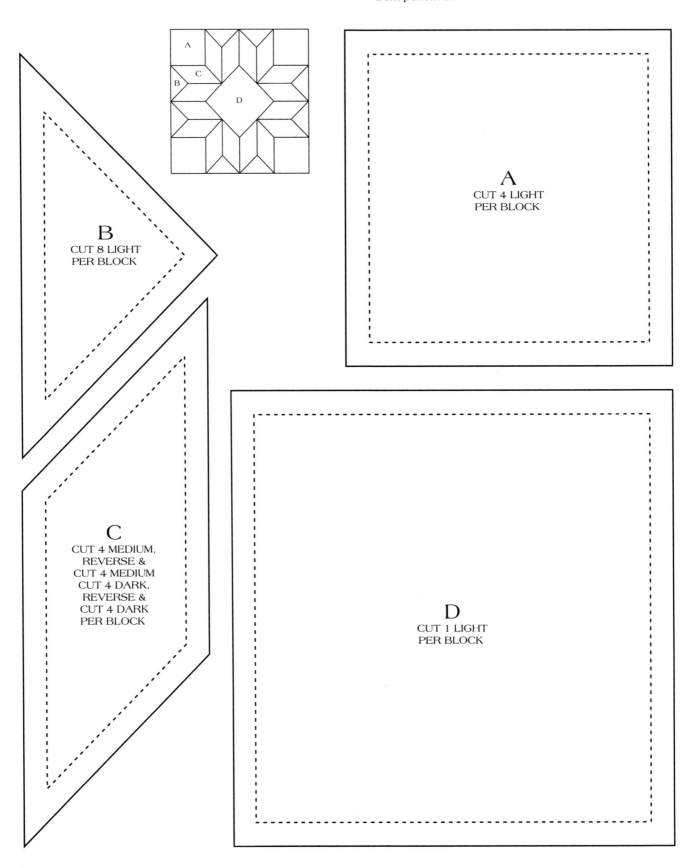

B
CUT 8 LIGHT
PER BLOCK

A
CUT 4 LIGHT
PER BLOCK

C
CUT 4 MEDIUM,
REVERSE &
CUT 4 MEDIUM
CUT 4 DARK,
REVERSE &
CUT 4 DARK
PER BLOCK

D
CUT 1 LIGHT
PER BLOCK

MINNESOTA Pattern Pieces

To make this block cut 8 medium and 8 dark triangles from pattern A. Cut 8 light triangles, reverse and cut 8 more from B. From C cut 4 medium color pieces. Cut 4 light triangles from pattern D. From pattern E cut 1 medium color square per block.

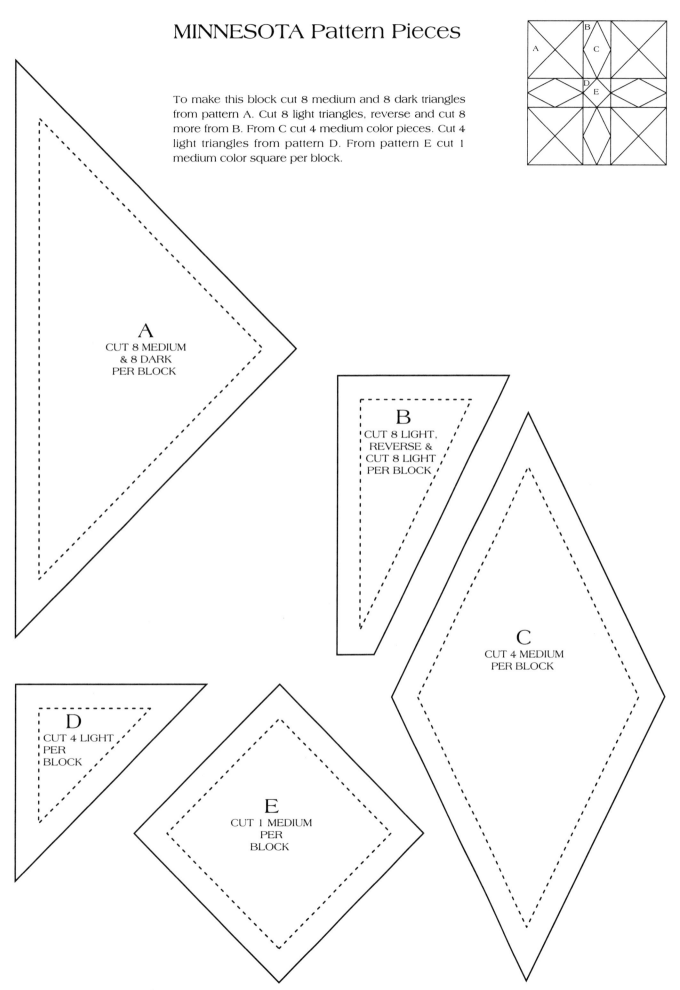

A
CUT 8 MEDIUM
& 8 DARK
PER BLOCK

B
CUT 8 LIGHT,
REVERSE &
CUT 8 LIGHT
PER BLOCK

C
CUT 4 MEDIUM
PER BLOCK

D
CUT 4 LIGHT
PER
BLOCK

E
CUT 1 MEDIUM
PER
BLOCK

MISSISSIPPI
Pattern Pieces

To make this block cut 4 light squares from pattern A. Cut 8 medium and 8 light color triangles from B. From C cut 4 light color pieces. Cut 4 medium-light triangles from pattern D. From pattern E cut 4 dark color pieces per block.

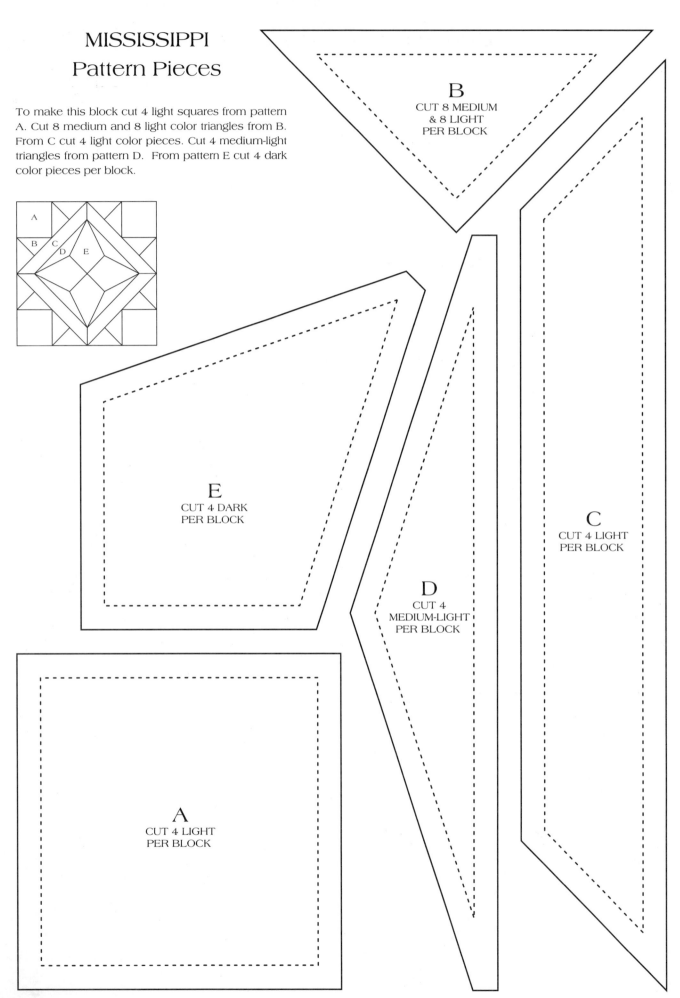

B
CUT 8 MEDIUM
& 8 LIGHT
PER BLOCK

E
CUT 4 DARK
PER BLOCK

C
CUT 4 LIGHT
PER BLOCK

D
CUT 4
MEDIUM-LIGHT
PER BLOCK

A
CUT 4 LIGHT
PER BLOCK

MISSOURI Pattern Pieces

To make this block cut 4 dark triangles from pattern A.
Cut 4 medium color pieces from B. From triangle C cut 4
light color pieces. Cut 8 dark triangles from pattern D.
From triangle E pattern cut 4 light and 4 medium color
pieces per block.

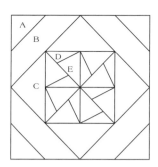

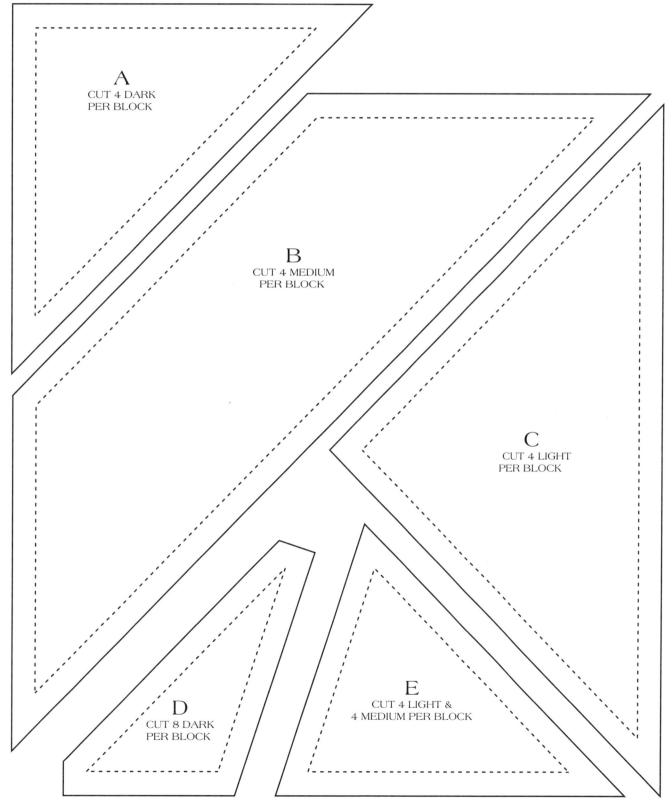

A
CUT 4 DARK
PER BLOCK

B
CUT 4 MEDIUM
PER BLOCK

C
CUT 4 LIGHT
PER BLOCK

D
CUT 8 DARK
PER BLOCK

E
CUT 4 LIGHT &
4 MEDIUM PER BLOCK

MONTANA Pattern Pieces

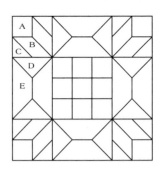

To make this block cut 9 dark and 4 light squares from pattern A. Cut 4 medium color pieces from B, reverse the pattern and cut 4 more medium color pieces from B. From triangle C cut 8 light color pieces. Cut 8 dark triangles from pattern D and 8 light color pieces from pattern E.

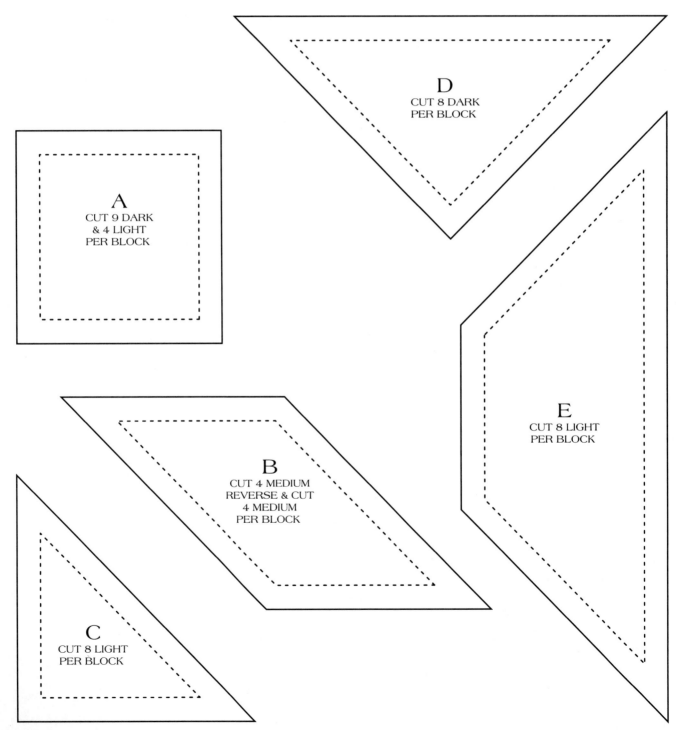

D
CUT 8 DARK
PER BLOCK

A
CUT 9 DARK
& 4 LIGHT
PER BLOCK

E
CUT 8 LIGHT
PER BLOCK

B
CUT 4 MEDIUM
REVERSE & CUT
4 MEDIUM
PER BLOCK

C
CUT 8 LIGHT
PER BLOCK

NEBRASKA Pattern Pieces

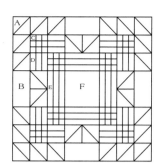

To make this block cut 28 dark, 8 medium, and 20 light pieces from triangle A. Cut 4 light pieces from rectangle B, and cut 40 dark and 32 light pieces from pattern C. From rectangle D cut 8 dark and 16 light pieces. Cut 4 dark, 4 medium, and 4 light pieces from rectangle E, and cut 1 light piece from square F.

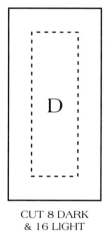

D

CUT 8 DARK
& 16 LIGHT
PER BLOCK

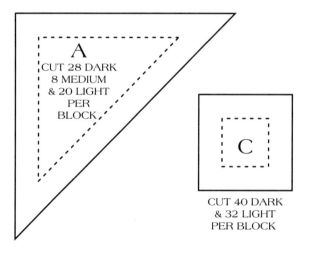

A

CUT 28 DARK
8 MEDIUM
& 20 LIGHT
PER
BLOCK

C

CUT 40 DARK
& 32 LIGHT
PER BLOCK

E
CUT 4 DARK, 4 MEDIUM & 4 LIGHT PER BLOCK

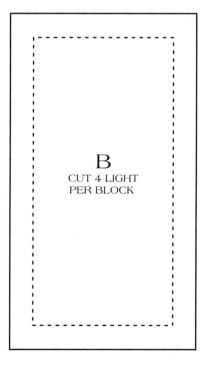

B
CUT 4 LIGHT
PER BLOCK

F
CUT 1 LIGHT PER BLOCK

To make this block cut 4 dark, reverse and cut 4 light color pieces from pattern A. Cut 8 light color triangles from pattern B. From C cut 1 light and 4 medium squares. Cut 4 light color D rectangles per block.

C

CUT 4 MEDIUM
& 1 LIGHT
PER BLOCK

A

CUT 4 DARK
REVERSE & CUT 4 LIGHT
PER BLOCK

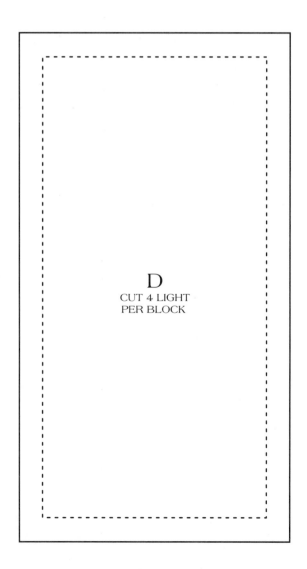

D

CUT 4 LIGHT
PER BLOCK

B

CUT 8 LIGHT
PER BLOCK

NEW HAMPSHIRE Pattern Pieces

To make this block cut 16 light color triangles from pattern A. Cut 4 medium color squares from pattern B. From C cut 4 dark, 2 light, and 2 medium pieces. Cut 1 dark color D square per block.

B
CUT 4 MEDIUM
PER BLOCK

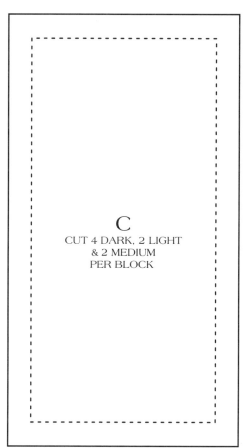

C
CUT 4 DARK, 2 LIGHT
& 2 MEDIUM
PER BLOCK

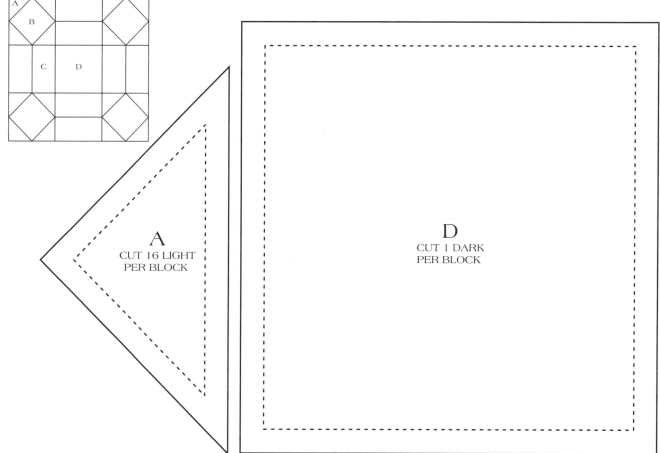

A
CUT 16 LIGHT
PER BLOCK

D
CUT 1 DARK
PER BLOCK

NEW JERSEY Pattern Pieces

To make this block cut 4 light color triangles from pattern A. Cut 8 dark color triangles from pattern B. From C cut 4 medium pieces. Cut 4 dark color D triangles per block. From E cut 4 light rectangles and from F cut 1 dark square per block.

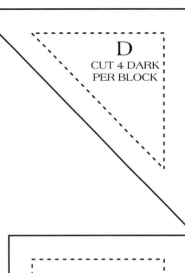

D
CUT 4 DARK
PER BLOCK

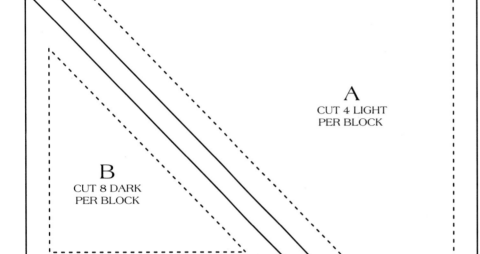

A
CUT 4 LIGHT
PER BLOCK

B
CUT 8 DARK
PER BLOCK

E
CUT 4 LIGHT
PER BLOCK

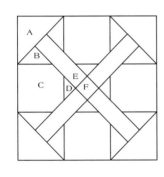

C
CUT 4 MEDIUM
PER BLOCK

F
CUT 1 DARK
PER BLOCK

NEW MEXICO Pattern Pieces

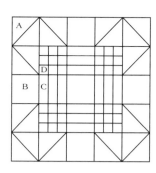

To make this block cut 12 dark and 12 light color triangles from pattern A. Cut 5 dark color squares from pattern B. From C cut 8 light and 4 dark rectangles. Cut 16 light and 20 dark color D squares per block.

A
CUT 12 DARK
& 12 LIGHT
PER BLOCK

D
CUT 16 LIGHT
& 20 DARK
PER BLOCK

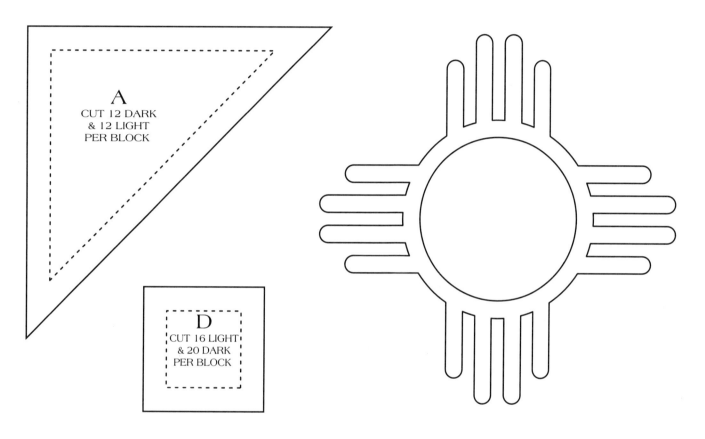

THE ANCIENT SUN SYMBOL
OF THE ZIA PUEBLO
WAS ADOPTED FOR
THE NEW MEXICO
STATE FLAG SYMBOL
IN 1925.

B
CUT 5 DARK
PER BLOCK

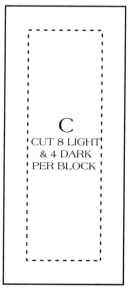

C
CUT 8 LIGHT
& 4 DARK
PER BLOCK

NEW YORK Pattern Pieces

To make this block cut 4 dark and 1 light color squares from pattern A. Cut 4 light color pieces from pattern B, reverse and cut 4 more light color pieces. From C cut 4 dark triangles. Cut 4 light and 5 medium D rectangles per block

A
CUT 4 DARK
& 1 LIGHT
PER BLOCK

B CUT 4 LIGHT,
REVERSE & CUT 4
MORE LIGHT
PER BLOCK

C
CUT 4 DARK
PER BLOCK

NEW YORK
STATE FLOWER
ROSE

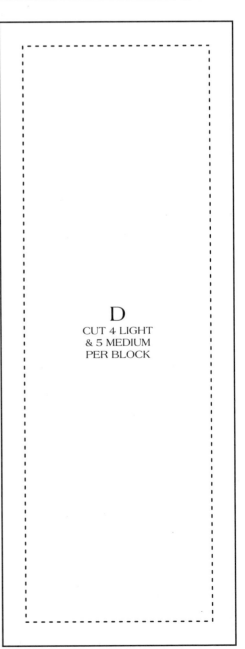

D
CUT 4 LIGHT
& 5 MEDIUM
PER BLOCK

NORTH CAROLINA Pattern Pieces

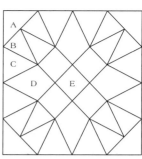

To make this block cut 4 medium color triangles from pattern A.
Cut 4 medium and 8 light color pieces from pattern B. From C
cut 8 light triangles. Cut 4 dark color D pieces per block. And
finally cut 1 dark and 4 light color squares from E per block.

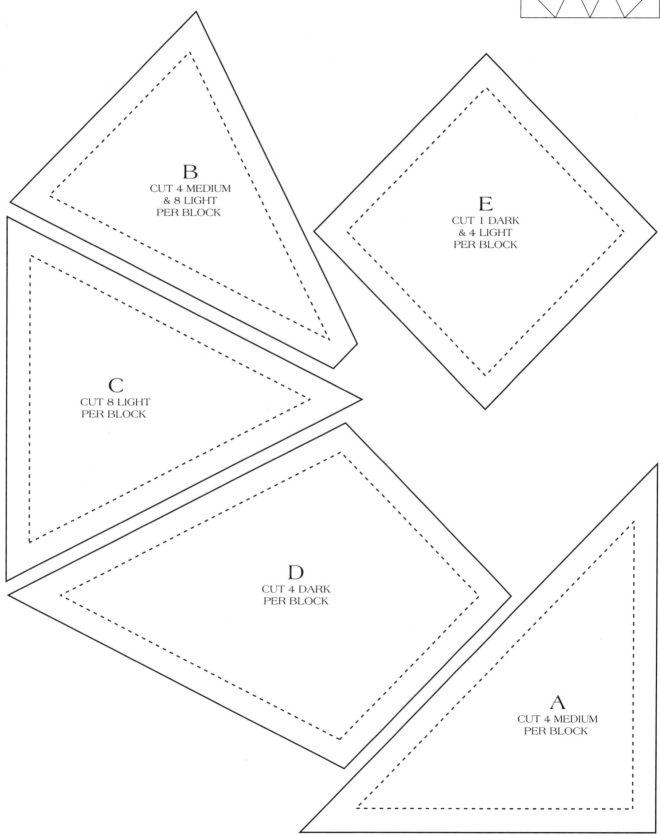

B
CUT 4 MEDIUM
& 8 LIGHT
PER BLOCK

E
CUT 1 DARK
& 4 LIGHT
PER BLOCK

C
CUT 8 LIGHT
PER BLOCK

D
CUT 4 DARK
PER BLOCK

A
CUT 4 MEDIUM
PER BLOCK

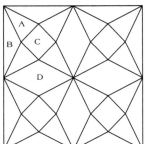

NORTH DAKOTA Pattern Pieces

To make this block cut 16 dark color pieces from pattern A. Cut 8 light B triangles and 4 medium C squares. Cut 4 light color D pieces per block.

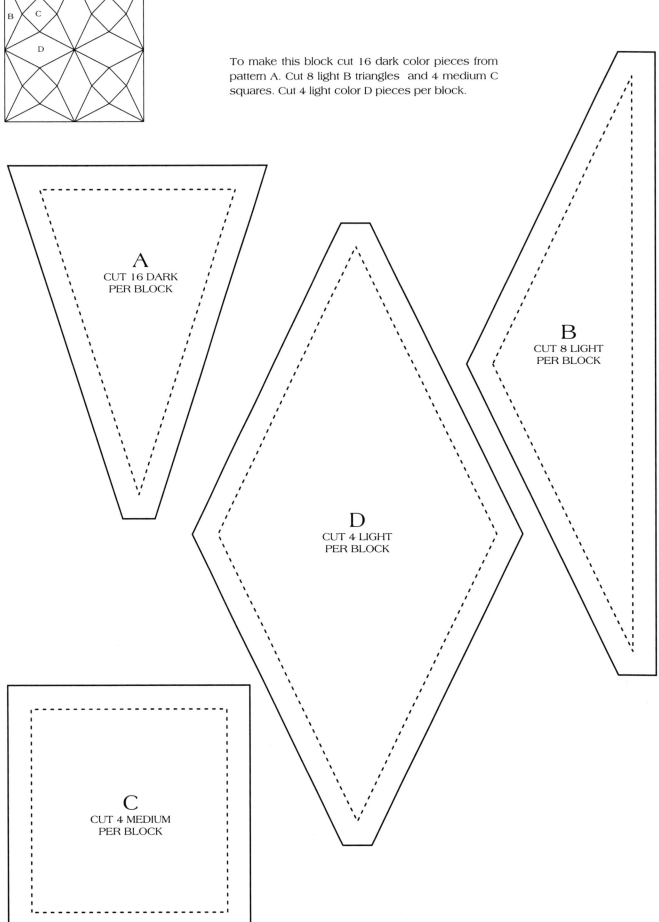

A
CUT 16 DARK
PER BLOCK

B
CUT 8 LIGHT
PER BLOCK

D
CUT 4 LIGHT
PER BLOCK

C
CUT 4 MEDIUM
PER BLOCK

OHIO Pattern Pieces

A			
B			

To make this block cut 2 light squares from pattern A. Cut 6 dark, 4 medium and 2 medium-light B rectangles per block.

OHIO STATE TREE
BUCKEYE TREE LEAF AND NUT

B
CUT 6 DARK, 4 MEDIUM
& 2 MEDIUM-LIGHT
PER BLOCK

A
CUT 2 LIGHT
PER BLOCK

OKLAHOMA Pattern Pieces

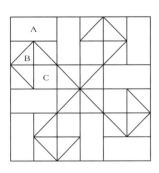

To make this block cut 8 light rectangles from pattern A.
Cut 16 light and 16 dark color pieces from pattern B.
From C cut 4 light squares per block.

B
CUT 16 LIGHT
& 16 DARK
PER BLOCK

C
CUT 4 LIGHT
PER BLOCK

OKLAHOMA STATE TREE
REDBUD LEAF

A
CUT 8 LIGHT
PER BLOCK

OREGON Pattern Pieces

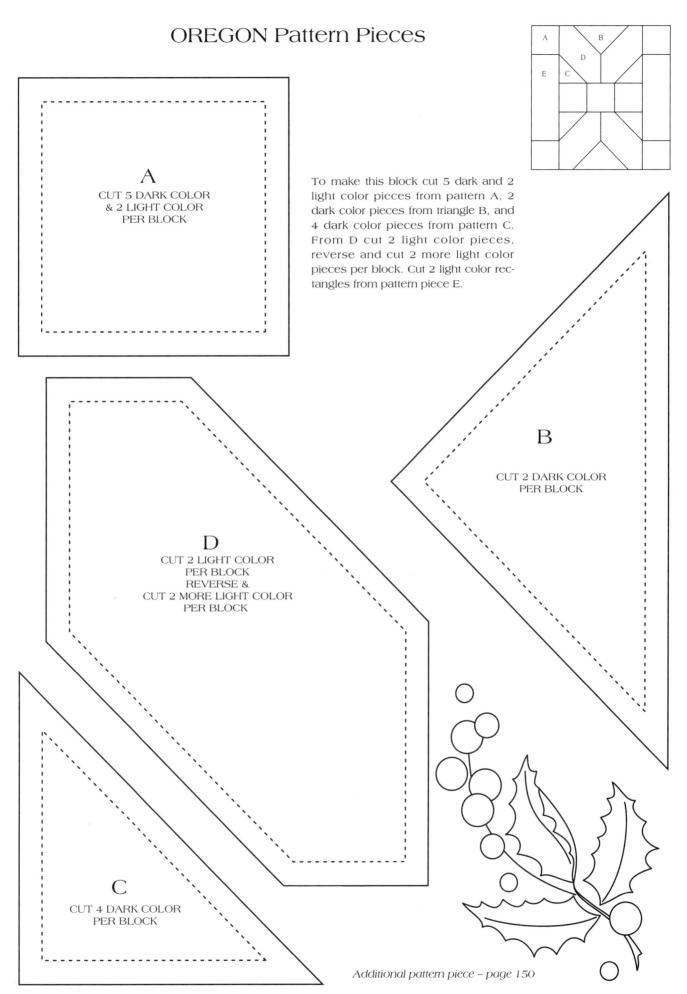

A
CUT 5 DARK COLOR
& 2 LIGHT COLOR
PER BLOCK

To make this block cut 5 dark and 2 light color pieces from pattern A, 2 dark color pieces from triangle B, and 4 dark color pieces from pattern C. From D cut 2 light color pieces, reverse and cut 2 more light color pieces per block. Cut 2 light color rectangles from pattern piece E.

B
CUT 2 DARK COLOR
PER BLOCK

D
CUT 2 LIGHT COLOR
PER BLOCK
REVERSE &
CUT 2 MORE LIGHT COLOR
PER BLOCK

C
CUT 4 DARK COLOR
PER BLOCK

Additional pattern piece – page 150

149

OREGON STATE FLOWER
THE HOLLY GRAPE

E

CUT 2 LIGHT COLOR
PER BLOCK

PENNSYLVANIA Pattern Pieces

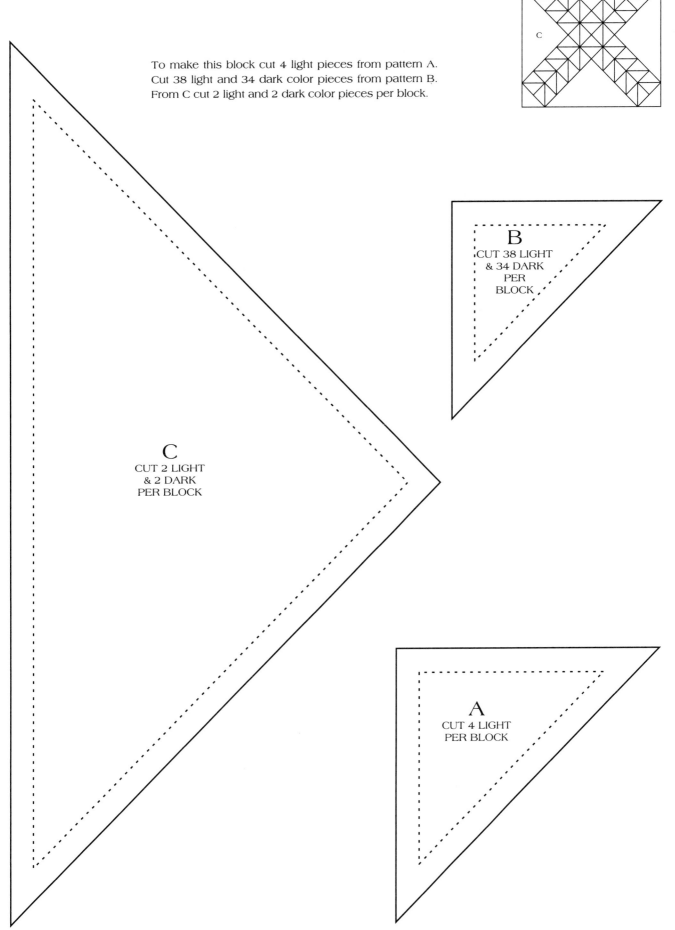

To make this block cut 4 light pieces from pattern A.
Cut 38 light and 34 dark color pieces from pattern B.
From C cut 2 light and 2 dark color pieces per block.

C
CUT 2 LIGHT
& 2 DARK
PER BLOCK

B
CUT 38 LIGHT
& 34 DARK
PER
BLOCK

A
CUT 4 LIGHT
PER BLOCK

151

RHODE ISLAND Pattern Pieces

To make this block cut 8 light and 8 dark pieces from pattern A. Cut 8 light color pieces from pattern B. From C cut 4 dark color pieces, reverse and cut 4 more dark color pieces. Cut 5 light color squares from D per block. From E cut 4 light color rectangles per block.

A
CUT 8 LIGHT
& 8 DARK
PER BLOCK

C
CUT 4 DARK
REVERSE & CUT
4 MORE DARK
PER BLOCK

RHODE ISLAND STATE TREE
RED MAPLE LEAF

B
CUT 8 LIGHT
PER BLOCK

D
CUT 5 LIGHT
PER BLOCK

E
CUT 4 LIGHT
PER BLOCK

SOUTH CAROLINA Pattern Pieces

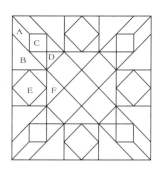

To make this block cut 4 light, reverse and cut 4 more light pieces from pattern A. Cut 8 medium color triangles from pattern B. From C cut 4 dark color square pieces. Cut 24 light and 4 medium color triangles from D per block. From E cut 5 dark and 4 light color squares, and from F cut 4 medium color triangles per block.

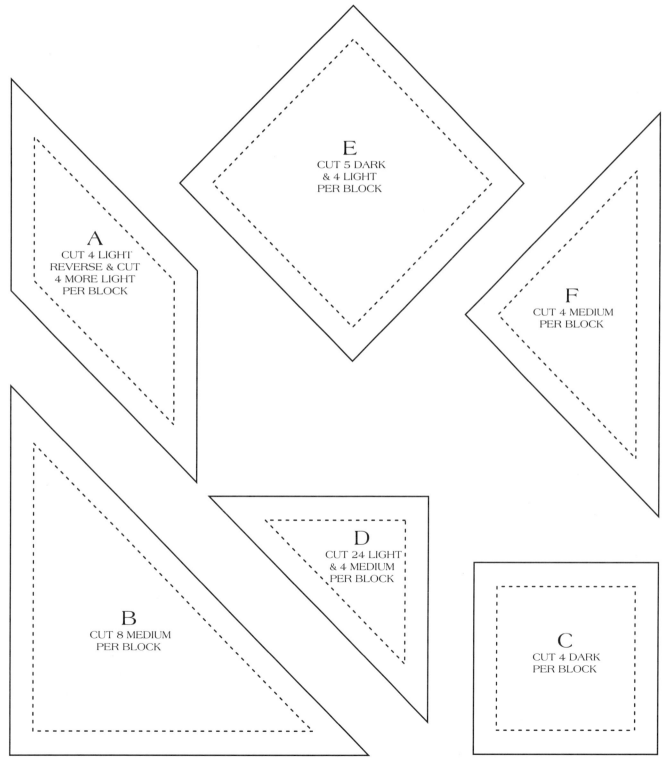

E
CUT 5 DARK
& 4 LIGHT
PER BLOCK

A
CUT 4 LIGHT
REVERSE & CUT
4 MORE LIGHT
PER BLOCK

F
CUT 4 MEDIUM
PER BLOCK

D
CUT 24 LIGHT
& 4 MEDIUM
PER BLOCK

B
CUT 8 MEDIUM
PER BLOCK

C
CUT 4 DARK
PER BLOCK

SOUTH DAKOTA Pattern Pieces

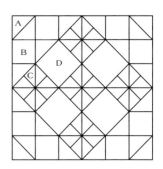

To make this block cut 6 light, 4 medium and 10 dark pieces from pattern A. Cut 8 light color squares from pattern B. From C cut 20 light and 20 medium color pieces. Cut 4 dark color squares from D per block.

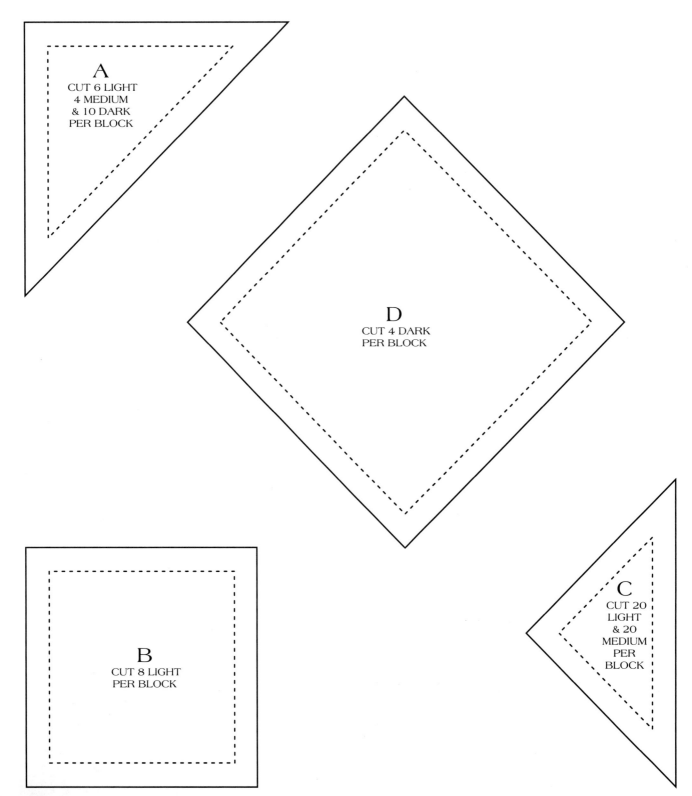

A
CUT 6 LIGHT
4 MEDIUM
& 10 DARK
PER BLOCK

D
CUT 4 DARK
PER BLOCK

B
CUT 8 LIGHT
PER BLOCK

C
CUT 20
LIGHT
& 20
MEDIUM
PER
BLOCK

TENNESSEE Pattern Pieces

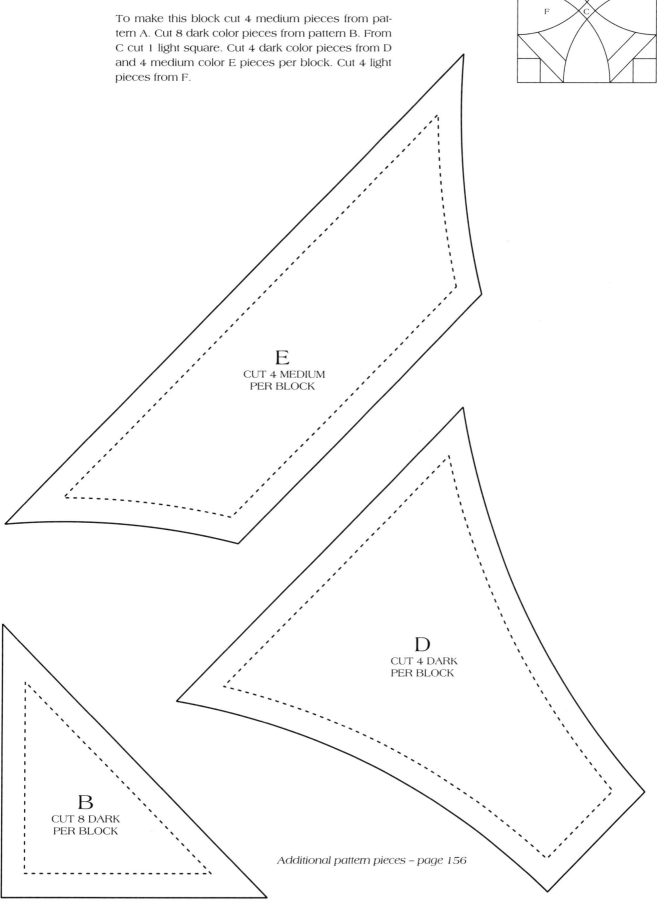

To make this block cut 4 medium pieces from pattern A. Cut 8 dark color pieces from pattern B. From C cut 1 light square. Cut 4 dark color pieces from D and 4 medium color E pieces per block. Cut 4 light pieces from F.

E
CUT 4 MEDIUM
PER BLOCK

D
CUT 4 DARK
PER BLOCK

B
CUT 8 DARK
PER BLOCK

Additional pattern pieces – page 156

A
CUT 4 MEDIUM
PER BLOCK

TENNESSEE Pattern Pieces

C
CUT 1 LIGHT
PER BLOCK

TENNESSEE STATE FLOWER
IRIS

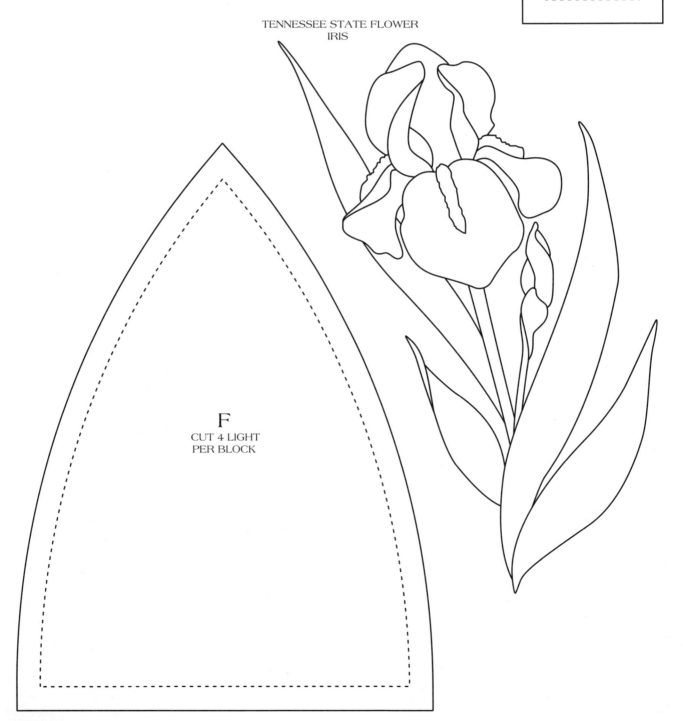

F
CUT 4 LIGHT
PER BLOCK

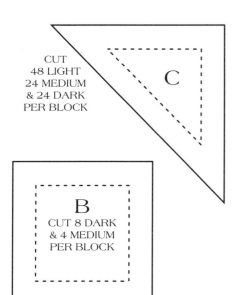

TEXAS Pattern Pieces

To make this block cut 4 light pieces from pattern A. Cut 8 dark and 4 medium color pieces from pattern B. From C cut 48 light, 24 medium, and 24 dark color pieces per block. Cut 4 light color pieces from D and 1 medium E square per block.

C
CUT
48 LIGHT
24 MEDIUM
& 24 DARK
PER BLOCK

B
CUT 8 DARK
& 4 MEDIUM
PER BLOCK

A
CUT 4 LIGHT
PER BLOCK

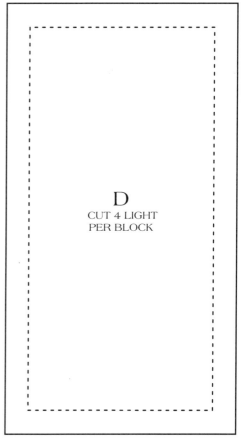

E
CUT 1 MEDIUM
PER BLOCK

D
CUT 4 LIGHT
PER BLOCK

UTAH Pattern Pieces

To make this block cut 12 light pieces from pattern A. From pattern B cut 8 light, reverse and cut 8 more light; cut 10 dark, reverse and cut 2 more dark; cut 2 medium, reverse and cut 2 more medium; then cut 8 medium-light making sure these medium-light pieces are the reverse of the 10 dark pieces.

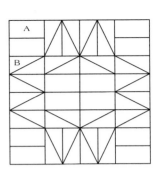

CUT 8 LIGHT, REVERSE & CUT 8 LIGHT
CUT 10 DARK, REVERSE & CUT 2 DARK
CUT 2 MEDIUM, REVERSE & CUT 2 MEDIUM
CUT 8 MEDIUM-LIGHT*
*Make sure these medium-light
pieces are reverse
of the 10 dark pieces

B

A
CUT 12 LIGHT
PER BLOCK

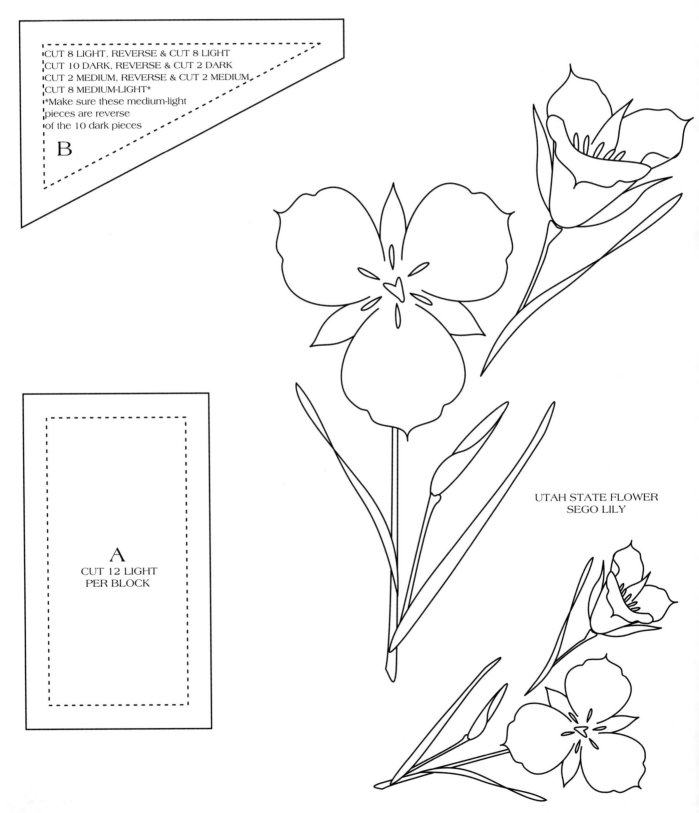

UTAH STATE FLOWER
SEGO LILY

VERMONT Pattern Pieces

To make this block cut 4 medium-dark pieces from pattern B. Cut 20 light, 14 dark and 14 medium color pieces from pattern A.

B
CUT 4 MEDIUM-DARK
PER BLOCK

A
CUT 20 LIGHT
14 MEDIUM
& 14 DARK
PER BLOCK

VERMONT STATE TREE
SUGAR MAPLE LEAF

VIRGINIA Pattern Pieces

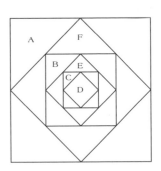

To make this block cut 2 light and 2 dark color pieces from pattern A. Cut 2 light and 2 dark color pieces from pattern B. Cut 2 light and 2 dark color pieces from pattern C. Cut 1 dark square from pattern D. Cut 2 light and 2 dark color pieces from pattern E, and 2 light and 2 dark color pieces from pattern F.

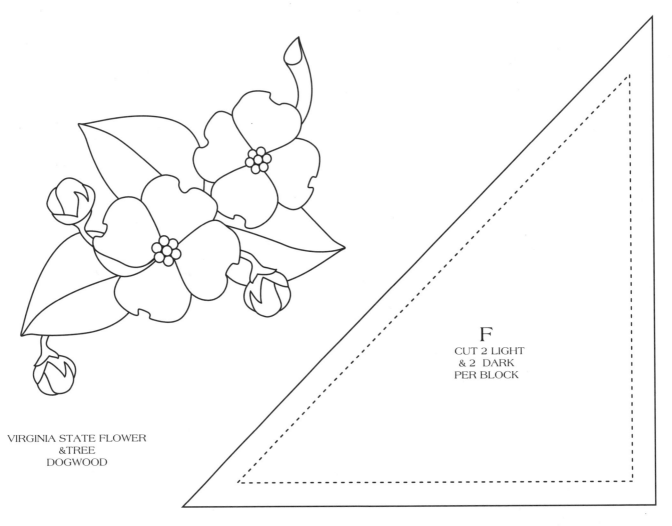

F
CUT 2 LIGHT
& 2 DARK
PER BLOCK

VIRGINIA STATE FLOWER
&TREE
DOGWOOD

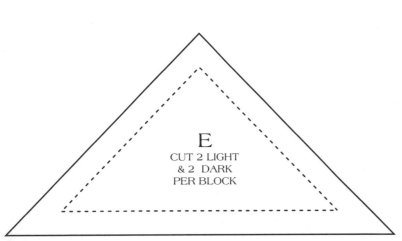

E
CUT 2 LIGHT
& 2 DARK
PER BLOCK

D
CUT 1 DARK
PER BLOCK

VIRGINIA Pattern Pieces

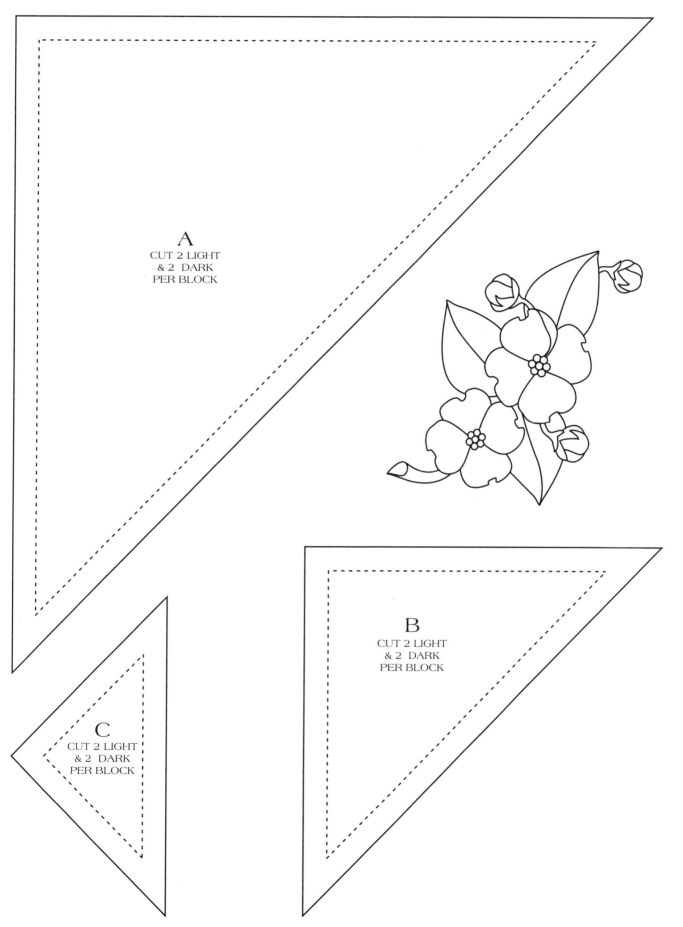

A
CUT 2 LIGHT
& 2 DARK
PER BLOCK

B
CUT 2 LIGHT
& 2 DARK
PER BLOCK

C
CUT 2 LIGHT
& 2 DARK
PER BLOCK

WASHINGTON Pattern Pieces

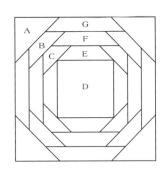

To make this block cut 4 light color pieces from pattern A. Cut 4 light pieces from pattern B and 4 light pieces from pattern C. Cut 1 light square from pattern D. From E, F, and G cut 4 dark color pieces each.

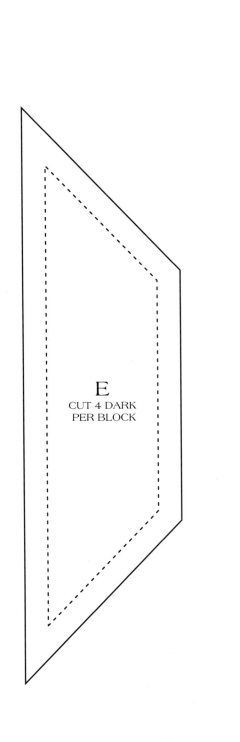

E
CUT 4 DARK
PER BLOCK

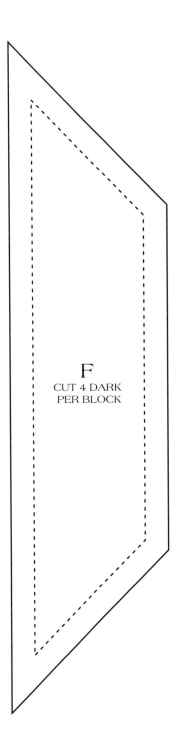

F
CUT 4 DARK
PER BLOCK

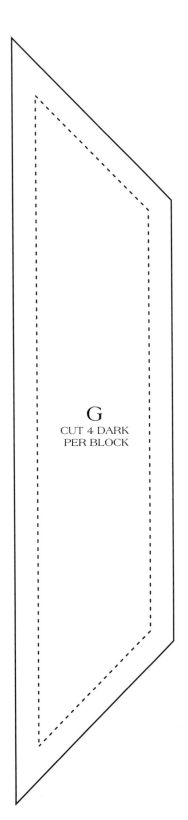

G
CUT 4 DARK
PER BLOCK

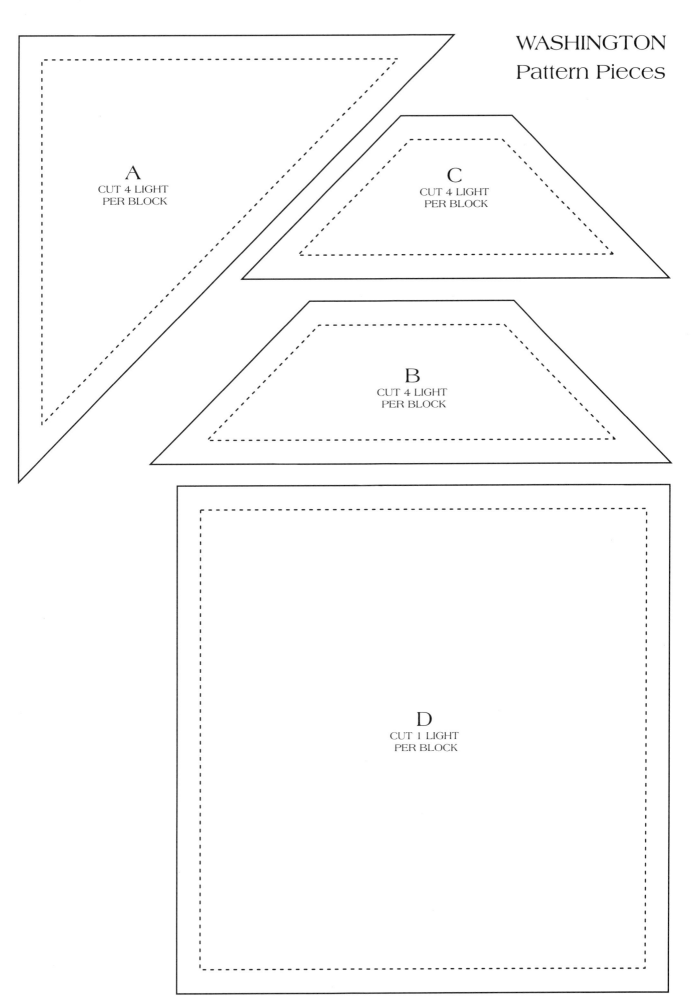

WASHINGTON
Pattern Pieces

A
CUT 4 LIGHT
PER BLOCK

C
CUT 4 LIGHT
PER BLOCK

B
CUT 4 LIGHT
PER BLOCK

D
CUT 1 LIGHT
PER BLOCK

WEST VIRGINIA Pattern Pieces

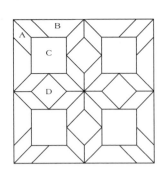

To make this block cut 8 light color pieces from pattern B. Cut 12 dark pieces, reverse and cut 12 medium color pieces from pattern A. Cut 4 light color pieces from pattern C and 4 light from D.

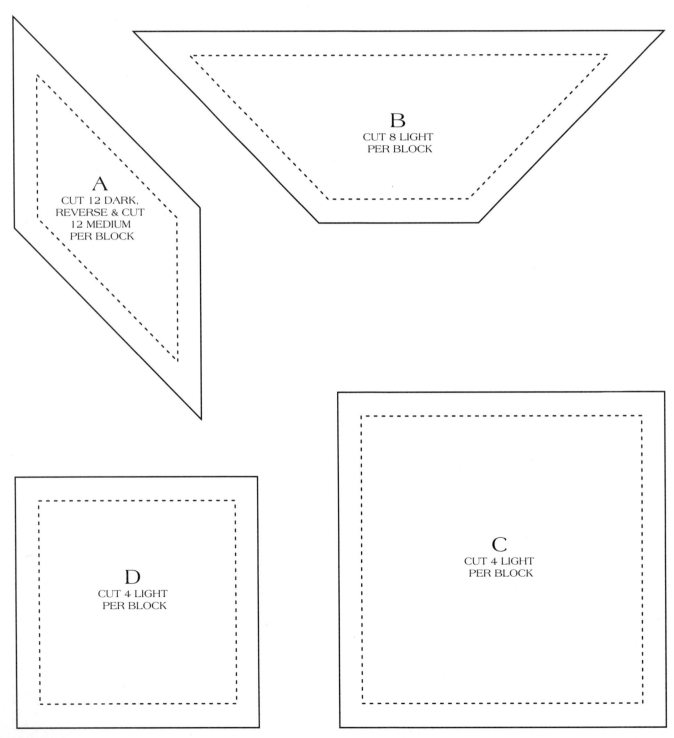

A
CUT 12 DARK,
REVERSE & CUT
12 MEDIUM
PER BLOCK

B
CUT 8 LIGHT
PER BLOCK

D
CUT 4 LIGHT
PER BLOCK

C
CUT 4 LIGHT
PER BLOCK

WISCONSIN Pattern Pieces

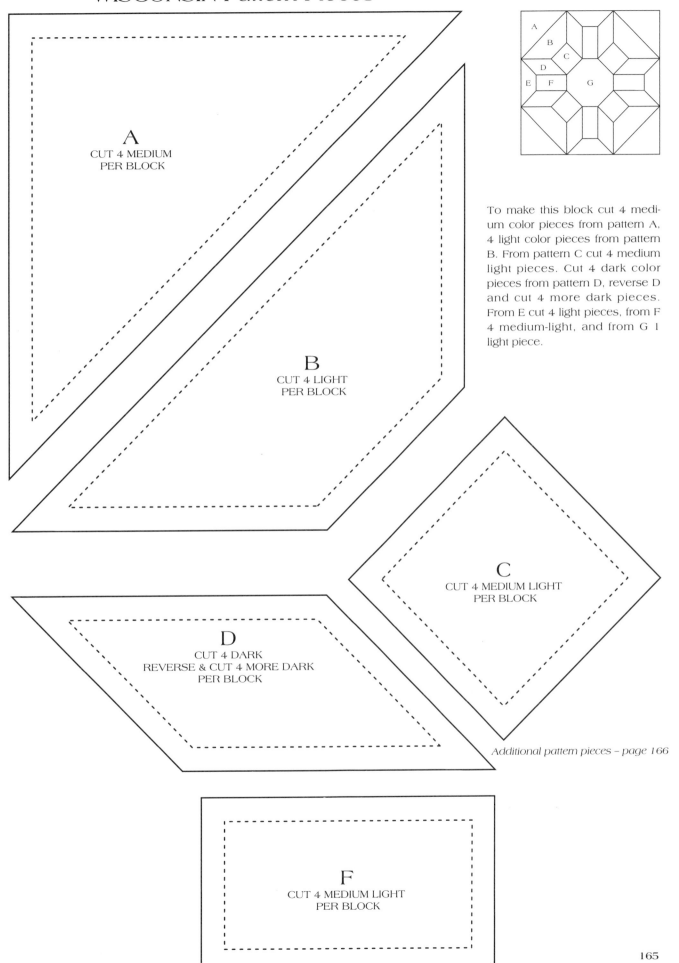

A
CUT 4 MEDIUM
PER BLOCK

B
CUT 4 LIGHT
PER BLOCK

C
CUT 4 MEDIUM LIGHT
PER BLOCK

D
CUT 4 DARK
REVERSE & CUT 4 MORE DARK
PER BLOCK

F
CUT 4 MEDIUM LIGHT
PER BLOCK

To make this block cut 4 medium color pieces from pattern A, 4 light color pieces from pattern B. From pattern C cut 4 medium light pieces. Cut 4 dark color pieces from pattern D, reverse D and cut 4 more dark pieces. From E cut 4 light pieces, from F 4 medium-light, and from G 1 light piece.

Additional pattern pieces – page 166

WISCONSIN Pattern Pieces

E
CUT 4 LIGHT
PER BLOCK

G
CUT 1 LIGHT
PER BLOCK

WISCONSIN STATE FLOWER
BIRD'S FOOT VIOLET

WYOMING Pattern Pieces

To make this block cut 4 light color pieces from pattern A; 28 light, 16 dark, and 16 medium color pieces from pattern B; and 1 light color piece from pattern C.

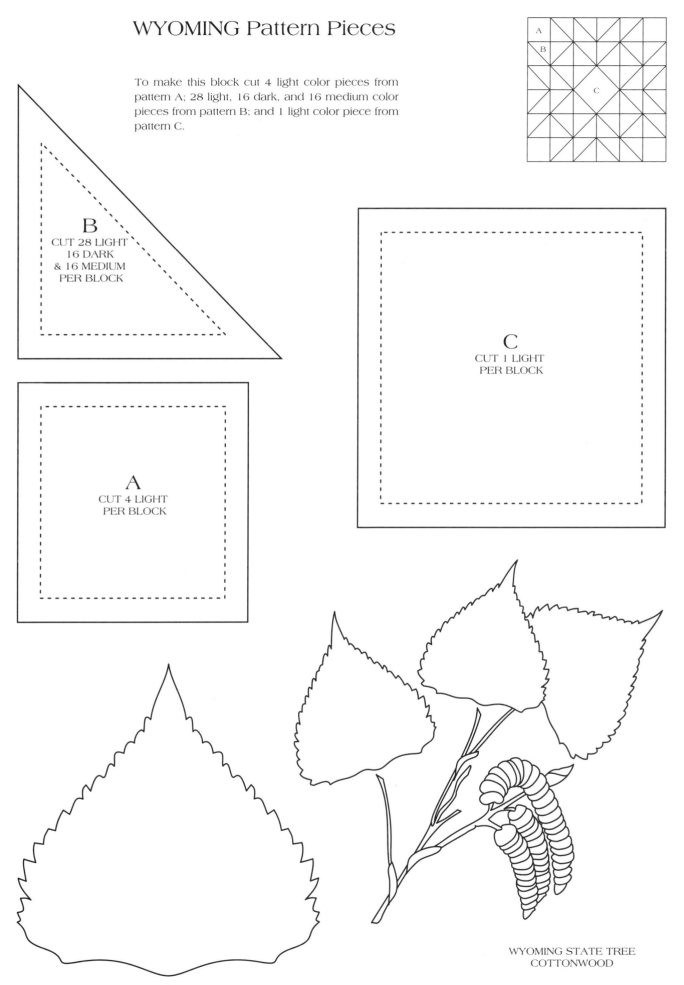

B
CUT 28 LIGHT
16 DARK
& 16 MEDIUM
PER BLOCK

C
CUT 1 LIGHT
PER BLOCK

A
CUT 4 LIGHT
PER BLOCK

WYOMING STATE TREE
COTTONWOOD

~ American Quilter's Society ~
dedicated to publishing books for today's quilters

These books can be found in local bookstores and quilt shops. If you are unable to locate a title in your area, you can order by mail from AQS, P.O. Box 3290, Paducah, KY 42002-3290.
Please add $2 for the first book and 40¢ for each additional one to cover postage and handling.
(International orders please add $2.50 for the first book and $1 for each additional one.)